# IN SEARCH
# OF THE NEW (III)

## DOCUMENTS OF AN ECUMENICAL ACTION /
## REFLECTION PROCESS ON NEW LIFE STYLES

Edited by Reinhild Traitler

Commission on the Churches' Participation in Development
150 rte. de Ferney – CH–1211 Geneva 20, Switzerland

## Acknowledgements

Carol Lunt edited the manuscript of the Gallneukirchen consultation and the address by Father Tissa Balasuriya. She also typed all the documents.

IDOC-Rome prepared the bibliography.

Daniel Caselli designed the cover.

ISBN 2-8254-0668-6

# CONTENTS

# INTRODUCTION

Soon after the Independent Commission on International Development Issues had begun its work in late 1977, a distinguished
African leader sent a message to its chairman, Willy Brandt, expressing the hope that this commission could "contribute to the
development of world-wide moral values."

This brief phrase outlines an ambitious endeavour: to develop
values commensurate with the hopes and expectations of communities, peoples and nations that would help to establish peace
on earth and possibilities for a humane life for present and
future generations; to anchor these values in the lives of
people; to consolidate them in adequate structures and institutions; and to develop a corresponding praxis.

In late 1975 the Commission on the Churches' Participation in
Development (CCPD) of the World Council of Churches initiated an
action/reflection process on "New Life Styles", following practical experiments launched by a number of churches in the wake of
the "energy crisis" of 1973. A new consciousness of the finite
nature of the planet's resources and of the uneven distribution
of the accumulated wealth of a few nations had prompted many
churches and communities in the rich nations to develop ways of
life that would allow a more just, participatory and sustainable
future for all. In a way the search for New Life Styles was a
quest for new values that could shape a better world. It was
also a search for a new spirituality that began to take shape in
the midst of the many efforts and struggles for a better world,
a rediscovery of the resources of faith and of the sustaining
power of communities.

During the Fifth Assembly of the WCC in Nairobi in 1975, two
basic lines were developed on the issue of New Life Styles. One
was related to the concern for the overall quality of life, particularly the quality of the threatened ecosphere. This prompted
a reflection on creation and the affirmation that the whole
creation shares the promise of ultimate redemption: Christians
are called to participate obediently in the work of "restoring
the whole creation".

A second line related to the life style of the churches and of
Christian communities, asking the churches to examine in particular how far their institutional life style was in line with
the gospel message "which brings judgement to the rich and hope
to the poor." "The church as a Christian community demonstrates
whose side it is on by the way it appears to its neighbours,"
the report of the section on "Education for Liberation and
Community" stated.

Both lines were developed further in the programmes of CCPD,
particularly in the study process on the Church and the Poor,
and in the programme on New Life Styles. A consultation was

1

organized in early 1977, bringing together new life styles groups and movements from North Atlantic countries which had already participated in the study process.

The consultation focused on practical experiences in the search for the new, on the relationship between personal efforts and necessary systemic changes, on the theological implications of new life styles efforts, and on the challenge they pose to rich churches.

The theological debate emphasized, in a new way, creation theology and the way the "dominion" over the earth, given to humankind, has been abused and perverted. Another theological insight offered by the consultation was that of the role of the poor in the economy of salvation. The orthodox concept of the sacrament of the poor pointed to the fact that the only way we can recognize and meet Christ is in service to those who are poor, despised, in prison, sick (Matt. 25). Indeed, St. John Chrysostomos in this context spoke about the "sacrament of the brother," and especially of the least among brothers, that is, the poor.

The consultation also looked at some practical experiences in the field of New Life Styles, particularly in communal living. Some criteria for evaluating such efforts were developed. An endeavour was made to assess in particular how such efforts can contribute to shaping a clearer vision of the new community. What new values and new modes of living could be applicable to the larger community which is not ready for radical experiments? For Christian communities this also includes the question of a new spirituality that emerges in concrete involvement and struggles for more justice.

The consultation further raised the question of how far systemic changes can be brought about by the various attempts at New Life Styles and how New Life Styles efforts need to be linked to systemic issues if they are to avoid being merely privatising affairs, only good for calming troubled minds. This question was raised on the basis of a number of experiences already going on in the field of New Life Styles. There were efforts to curb consumption and to save energy; there were efforts to exercise solidarity with the poor in the Third World by transferring the resources thus saved; there were efforts to raise environmental issues (which signify a problem of inter-generational justice), ranging from the debate on nuclear energy to efforts to return to the land, to live in harmony with nature, etc.

The consultation then listed a variety of areas in which New Life Styles movements can work on necessary systemic changes, and made a variety of suggestions as to how the personal style of life could be changed to allow for fuller participation of all members of society in the total decision-making process.

The reflection on "New Life Styles and Systemic Change" indicated a basic dilemma of the whole action/reflection process: how to indicate the specificity of what is meant by New Life Styles and how to establish the links between personal or small group efforts and the type of political impulses that are necessary to bring about structural changes.

The consultation appointed a small core group to continue the action/reflection process on New Life Styles. The task of the group was to accompany ongoing new life styles efforts in a number of countries, and to relate to projects at the international level (such as the UN University project on Alternative Ways of Life). This core group met twice, in November 1977 and September 1979. It kept contact with many efforts and groups and developed a number of resources (three Dossiers were published on the issue of New Life Styles).

During its first meeting the core group singled out three issues:

- It firmly placed the search for the new in the context of the search for a more just, participatory and sustainable society. In this context all efforts are part of a global search for the new, though this has different implications at different levels.

- It asked that more meaning be given to the concept of solidarity with the poor and their struggles as an important element of New Life Styles and expressed its conviction that real changes towards a just, participatory and sustainable society would come through the inner strength of the poor who, with their struggles ... create the basis for the future society.

- It considered efforts at New Life Styles as the creation within present-day society of free spaces where the values of a just, participatory and sustainable society begin to be realized. They are "liberated zones, to be continuously widened and extended," where new values are emerging and new forms of organization can be experimented with.

Based on this assessment, the group decided to give priority to studying the links between systemic change and efforts at "personal liberation" experienced in many new life styles efforts. IDOC was asked to prepare a dossier on this issue, and the work of the group served also as input for the report to the Programme Unit on Justice and Service Committee of the WCC Central Committee, meeting in Jamaica in 1979.

The report to Central Committee pointed to a number of problem areas which had been identified:

- One was the fact that new life styles efforts were, by and large, concentrated in certain sectors of the middle classes of affluent societies. Some studies had shown that lower income groups usually rejected the idea of new life styles, particularly when emphasis was put on reducing consumption.

- Another problem was how to influence patterns of production. Serious alternatives in economic organization would only emerge if the content of production could be changed. The possibility of influencing production from the consumer's angle, however, was rather limited. "As long as decision making on production remains in the hands of a powerful few, the law of free enterprise and the free market will be more important than the law of justice for all," the document stated.

3

- Another problem related to ongoing efforts at New Life Styles
was that, on the whole, they declined to work through established institutions. How, it was asked, can such a movement
avoid marginalization? And isn't the movement demanding that
"systemic changes come about solely by moral persuasion"?

Based on this progress report, the Central Committee of the WCC,
at its meeting in Jamaica in 1979, asked CCPD to pay special
attention to the contributions of churches in the Third World to
the issue of New Life Styles, especially in terms of developing
alternatives to current concepts of development. It also asked
that special emphasis be put on the relationship between systemic
change and personal liberation, on questions of influencing production, and on the search for new values.

Based on the recommendations of the core group, which met again
in September 1979, CCPD decided to organize a Consultation on
New Life Styles to bring the present phase of the action/reflec-
tion process to an end and to advise CCPD as to how to present
the insights gained to the member churches of the WCC. On the
recommendation of the WCC Central Committee, representatives of
CCPD partners in the Third World were invited to this meeting,
which made for a completely new dynamic in the discussion of the
issue, placing it more firmly within the search for "another
development". It became clear that New Life Styles, taken
seriously, are really a call for another development based on
different goals, for a people-centred and people-promoted
development. The consultation took place in May 1980 in
Gallneukirchen, Austria.

In the following we present the reports of the two consultations
organized as part of the action/reflection process on New Life
Styles and the report of the November 1977 meeting of the Core
Group. An in-depth bibliography prepared by IDOC-Rome, and one
of the keynote addresses given at the Consultation in Gallneukirchen complement these reports. We hope these materials will
provide resources for a continuing process of reflection and
action in the churches. The search for the new must not stop
here. It has only just begun.

Commission on the Churches'
Participation in Development
January 1981.

# CONSULTATION ON NEW LIFE STYLES

## GALLNEUKIRCHEN

### MAY 4 - 10, 1980

# I. THE PROCESS OF THE CONSULTATION

People from 17 different countries in all five continents came together in Gallneukirchen, Austria, from May 4 to 10, 1980, in order to continue the action/reflection process by the Commission on the Churches' Participation in Development on the issues raised by new life styles movements in various parts of the world.

We shared our life and work during these days together, we shared our commitments and struggles to bring about a more just, participatory and sustainable future for all God's children, we prayed and sang, and we felt that, in a small way, we were anticipating the liberated community of the new heaven and the new earth. In the presentations of the struggles of groups all over the globe for a more humane world it became clear to us that, in spite of conflicts, differences and ambiguities, we are part of a movement which is emerging from the bonds of captivity, a movement which is trying to affirm the life abundant for all of humanity.

On the basis of the national presentations, Dr. Jan Pronk of the Netherlands addressed the group on the economic and political issues facing the world at the beginning of the eighties. He drew our attention to the interrelatedness of all processes of life on earth, and to the precarious predicament of a world characterized by tremendous inequalities and intensifying power struggles. He also made it clear that those scenarios for the future developed so far hardly take any account of the hopes, aspirations and struggles for alternatives of the poor majority of the world.

Fr. Tissa Balasuriya called for a process of repentance and conversion among Christians and churches: the churches' complicity in the process of barbaric conquest, intervention and exploitation that has gone on for centuries and still continues needs to be acknowledged. Hope today emerges from the masses of the poor and oppressed peoples: their oppression is forcing them to struggle for a radically different future and in their struggles we can perceive God's work in history, the unfolding of His Kingdom where there will be "life abundant" for all of humanity. This raises the question of the authenticity of mission which originates in the rich nations and is directed to the poor majority, from whose continuing starvation and misery the mission-sending countries draw much of their affluence and welfare. It further raises the question of the relationship of the institutional churches to the ecclesial communities emerging in the people's struggles - their witness, their way of life, their spirituality and their commitment to live out a gospel that is "good news to the poor".

In our group work we tried to deepen some of these issues: our reflections are presented in the following report.

During the consultation we met with Superintendent Dr. L. Temmel of the Upper Austria Diocese of the Evangelical Church (A.u. H B) in Austria, and with representatives of the Quaker community of Linz. We shared some of our insights and heard about the situation of Protestantism in Austria. We also visited Martinstift, a home for mentally handicapped children run by the Diakonisches Werk of the protestant church, and learned about the exemplary work of the church with these least of our brothers and sisters in Christ. In addition, some of us participated in the peace march organized on May 9 by some alternative groups in the area of Linz.

On May 8, the "Gallneukirchner Stubenmusik", a group of people who are reviving old Austrian folk music, spent an evening with us. We listened to the beauty of the people's music, created around the idea of harmony, and participated in the singing, discovering for ourselves how difficult and exacting it is to achieve harmony. We were grateful for this opportunity to discover once again the strength of the people's culture and its power to build and sustain community.

We want to extend our thanks to the staff of the "Waldheimat", a guest house and rehabilitation centre for retarded girls. We thank Ms. Garbeis and Sister Gertraud Novak, the directors of the Diakonisches Werk, Pastor Cepek and Pastor Gäbler, and last but not least all the girls who served us with smiles and patience.

Perhaps the most significant outcome of the time we spent at Gallneukirchen was the feeling of solidarity with each other – people from different cultures, able to come together with a common purpose, not only to share their struggles but also to rejoice in the knowledge that hope is present, that in the new life of people and their movement there is anticipation of the Kingdom of God.


## II. THE CONTEXT AND FOCUS OF EFFORTS FOR NEW LIFE STYLES

"You've got business in Boston, want a suite in the Seychelles, a car in Kuwait, a weekend in the West End, but right now, your're in conference in the Caribbean. Who cares?" ran a recent ad in Newsweek International. "WE care," it continued, featuring a seductively smiling air hostess, as if she were able to meet all the "basic needs" of the jet set of the globe, whilst a weary executive relaxed in the Caribbean sun. The ad is the epitome of a profit, consumption and pleasure oriented society, the smallness and interdependence of spaceship earth, the spirit of conquest of those who rule it, and the speed with which global interventions have become possible. It shows women as objects in the commercial sphere, with men carrying responsibility and making decisions. The poor and oppressed, whose labour makes possible the lavish and wasteful life style of the rich, are not even mentioned. They have no buying power, their style of life is not very orderly and their lives are daily struggles for survival. It is difficult to "care" for them. It is easier, and certainly more profitable, to care for the rich.

The cynicism of this scrap of commercial communication is a forceful illustration of the unprecedented situation in which the global human community finds itself as it moves towards the end of the twentieth century. During the last decade it has become clear that all life processes today, no matter how local they may be, have global implications. The internationalization of capital, in the wake of the expansion and pervasion of transnational corporations in all parts of the world, has created a link-up of power structures which are maintained by political, military and technological mechanisms. Economic and social structures focus on creating means of profit maximization. Few societies have been able to develop economies in which people matter, though we realize that socialist societies, by and large, have done better in overcoming glaring social and economic inequalities. Military potential has increased to a higherto unknown extent in order to maintain superpower hegemonies and contain people's aspirations and struggles for a different, life-oriented future. The overkill capacity of known arsenals is sufficient to wipe out the human race many times over, and the ever-expanding arms race continues to waste scarce resources and energy and to absorb the creativity of large sectors of the scientific community. A culture of violence, preoccupation with conflict scenarios, and brutal exploitation of the poor and powerless make abundantly clear to what extent many societies today are built on the power of death and destruction rather than on the affirmation of life for all.

When we turn to the scenarios for the future that have been developed so far we do not see much reason for hope. Most are engineered by élites. With the exception of the "Third System" project of the International Foundation for Development Alternatives, none of the major scenarios takes into account the voice of the poor and oppressed majority of the world's population, the hopes they have, the alternatives they are trying to work out.

There is a tendency among the world's economic planners, political leaders and futurists to look at the international situation with a certain degree of apprehension and pessimism. They see the end of an era and feel the need to re-arrange the international order. The most enlightened among them fear the violence with which the mighty and powerful might react to any change in the situation; they are afraid that once again the response of the stronger countries will be to victimize the weaker. Consequently the scenarios now being developed for the future reflect the preoccupation of the rich to maintain and defend their present level of affluence and position of power and to shift the burden resulting from their accumulative wealth to the weakest groups, both nationally and internationally. At best these scenarios make a moral appeal to the rich to share some of their wealth. At worst they outline grim struggles for the global distribution of scarce resources. They make it clear that the rich consider it their birthright to remain rich and that the poor had better not raise their voice in anger and despair, lest there be global conflict of unprecedented dimensions.

Opposed to this tone of apprehension, there is the vision of nations and peoples rising up after centuries of deep slumber to claim their due as equals in dignity and rights. The decline of the long heyday of domination when the West had the whole human race and the entire earth at its service might explain the pessimism felt among the mighty and powerful. But listening and responding to the aspirations of the oppressed peoples and races,

marginalized cultures and despised religions, and even to the more
sensitive voices among their own prophets, workers, youth and
women, can lead towards their own liberation and humanization.
It will help them to understand that they have to be cut to size,
that their life style cannot be built, maintained and ensured
for future generations on the basis of continuing exploitation
and extermination of other peoples and of nature itself.

As Christians who live with the promise of Jesus Christ, whose
Kingdom is life abundant for all of humanity, we cannot remain
silent in the face of this situation. We need first of all to
affirm, in word and in action, the power of life over death, the
power of resurrection over the powers that enslave, exploit and
destroy. We are all holding on to the thin thread of life. This
bonds people everywhere together, whether in the north or in the
south. In the underdeveloped countries it is death by starvation
that snaps the thread of life; in the developed countries, death
by destruction of the ecosystem. The victims of hunger and the
victims of pollution are the same. The mechanisms of exploitation are the same. The values that allow sweated labour in
Third World free trade zones, that advertize cheap prostitution
in exotic tourist destinations and that consider compensation to
victims cheaper than clearance of toxic waste dumping sites are
the same. In all cases death and destruction carry more weight
than the affirmation of life for all and respect for the sanctity
of human life.

Many new life styles efforts have tried in a variety of ways to
affirm life in the midst of a death culture. They have tried to
struggle against economic growth at the expense of the quality
and safety of human life. They have struggled against nuclear
power, pollution and the shifting of pollution and toxic waste to
Third World countries. They have struggled for the right to life
and to cultural expression of minorities; they have struggled to
overcome spiritual poverty and alienation in affluent consumer
societies by voluntarily reducing consumption and by experimenting
with new forms of communal living. They have made efforts to
develop a non-violent alternative culture, based on the people's
own cultural and creative resources; they have tried to develop
alternatives in a variety of fields, from health care to agriculture, marketing, education, etc., with a view to overcoming
the fragmentation of society created by the ever-increasing imposed division of labour. In fact new life styles movements have
found a wide variety of expression and have made it possible for
people who otherwise have no access to power to participate effectively in a wide spectrum of social and political processes at
local and national levels.

The manifold expressions of new life styles movements are not always without ambiguities. Some new life styles efforts merely
serve as an escape from the political actions necessary to provide
a new way of life for all. They may create comfortable hideaways
far removed from responsibilities and be interested only in the
building up of individuals and small groups. However, many efforts are placed within the wider framework of the search for a
different future, based on justice, participation and sustainability. We want to affirm that this framework is indispensable
for any effort which aims to contribute to the creation of a
viable future for all.

10

Our analysis has shown that most efforts in Third World societies
tend to move from a global socio-political analysis to sectorial
activities which are considered necessary and feasible steps on
the way to a global political alternative. On the other hand,
most movements in the developed countries start to organize around
sectorial issues (environment, nuclear energy, communal living,
peace movement, alternatives in consumption, health, education,
etc.) and usually move towards awareness of the various symptoms
of the system and attempts at a global analysis of the root
causes. In all cases life styles movements have a tremendous
potential to be people's movements, struggling for justice, participation and sustainability.

In the light of this anaysis we became convinced that the term
"new life styles" is a misleading description of the type of
struggles in which many new life styles movements are involved.
It suggests a fashion to be quickly changed, whereas in reality
the movements are involved in a protracted struggle. It also
suggests possibilities of individual action, whilst the movements
have made it clear that what they are about is a collective
effort which demands discipline and sacrifice. When we talk about
new life styles we mean <u>people's struggles for the creation of an
alternative future</u> based on the affirmation of life for all and
grounded in the principles of justice, participation and the sustainability of the earth.

New styles of life, new values and new organizations of personal,
communal and social life are emerging in the struggles of the
people for a new, more humane future. In this context the
people's movements must continue to raise the concern for new
life styles within the wider framework of structural changes; to
keep the revolution human is an ongoing task. Mechanisms of oppression are usually deeply embedded in cultural and social norms
and habits, and are not automatically overcome once the structures of domination have been changed. The creation of a new
person, a new humanity, where there is truly "neither Greek nor
Jew, neither man nor woman, neither freeman nor slave", but
where all are free, responsible and responsive persons is a long
process that requires daily struggle. It is indeed a spiritual
problem that cannot be solved solely through a change in the
material conditions of our personal and collective lives.

The people's movements have a unique opportunity to anticipate
the future, both in their political actions and struggles and in
their personal and collective lives. They can be signs, however
small and fragile, of a different world, free spaces where new
values take shape, new styles of life are experimented with,
alternative ways of organization are worked out and networks of
solidarity are established across barriers of nation state, race,
sex and religion. They can also be places where a new, radical
response to the challenge of the gospel takes shape, where ecclesial communities emerge in the struggle of people who try to
live out faith, hope and love in the face of the "principalities
and powers".

Finally, people's movements must help make transparent the development of future scenarios and bring the aspirations of the poor
and oppressed masses into the process of planning the future.

11

This is fundamentally a political task and requires from the movements that they make efforts to overcome their own fragmentation and perceive their issue-oriented work as part of the wider struggle towards a more just, participatory and sustainable world.

## III. SIGNS OF HOPE

### A. Trends, emerging values and attitudes

We live in a period of struggle, and thus in a time of transition. In the struggle for a new world order, new values are emerging from people's movements and groups committed to the building of a more just society. In their experiences, the objectives for which they are fighting, the mechanisms of the struggle, the way of life of the group and the basic attitudes of the individuals are closely linked. What is emerging from their variety is a new value system which, though still embryonic, is tending to replace the established system of values which is felt to be dehumanizing and oppressive.

Thus, while individualistic attitudes prevail in societies which are based on authoritarian, hierarchical and bureaucratic values, the groups committed to change tend to gather in communities and collectives, making people's participation, horizontal communications and shared leadership the basis of their action. They are marked by a strong sense of justice and, reacting against the general tendency of "minding one's own business", they see themselves as advocates for the powerless. In a cynical society where the human body and person are considered as objects, to the extent of glorifying death and violence and tolerating, with only superficial indignation and little forceful condemnation, phenomena such as sexual assaults and rape, people's movements demonstrate a great sensitivity and openness to others which allow them to understand from within the suffering and problems of their neighbour. The reality of sisterhood developed by the women's movement as well as the brotherhood and comradeship among members of people's movements are antidotes to the isolation into which the world is pushing us and give strength for the struggle. There is in these movements a deep respect for life, an acceptance of others in their otherness.

At the same time, however, they do not try to escape the contest against the forces of destruction and death. They know it is a conflict which will require of them a strong sense of discipline and great sacrifice. In this, they distinguish themselves from the false prophets who preach "peace, peace while there is no peace" and from a society which is determined to satisfy its greed and pleasure, no matter what the cost. In the family the sharing of tasks and of parenthood itself, as a reaction against patriarchy, are ways of implementing at the micro level the un-hierarchical and non-authoritarian approach demanded at the level of the whole of society and of education to overcome sexism, racism and other forms of discrimination present in society.

12

This whole value system, already present in the movements but not yet realized in society at large, indicates how much more human is the world envisioned by people's movements and movements for change. These movements are contesting the lack of humanity of the present set up not only by their theory or ideology, not only by their action, but also by their whole way of life. They are in themselves a sign of hope; the hope that comes out of coherent commitment to a clear objective, the hope that arises from the struggle. By their very life style they are defeating the resignation and passivity so common in our world today. The value system which is emerging points to a people on the move, a people more interested in being and sharing than in having and keeping. They are a people on the way towards a promised land, searching for the new, not a people on the defensive, building walls out of fear of losing what they have, whose latest monstrous creations are the national security states built up by today's dictatorships.

To practise these values in our everyday life is a continuous struggle. We have to fight against principalities and powers, against the mentality diffused by the mass media, against the cycle of production and consumption which creates artificial needs and manipulates real ones. We have to fight against building patterns of behaviour based on feudal customs and commercial values, against the fragmentation of a society in which social responsibilities have been removed from the total community to specialized institutions. This fragmentation is reflected in the variety of movements themselves. In the north, the so-called "welfare state" encourages consumerism and contains protest and, if it is true that in these societies the lower strata are made to carry the burden of the crisis, it must also be affirmed that whatever security and affluence is distributed by the "welfare state" is based on exploitation of the Third World. Theologically, we have to fight against an individualistic notion of sin and salvation.

## B. A theological reflection

### 1. On the values of the Gospel

The Gospel radically challenges established norms and values. The way of Jesus, the annunciation of the Kingdom in our very midst, is a powerful contestation against all those norms that enslave, oppress and dehumanize people. In his encounter with the Pharisees, Jesus called into question a law that held people captive; in his encounters with women he affirmed the dignity and equality of women, whose social position in Hebrew society was characterized by inequality and degradation. In his ministry with the outcasts of his time - the ill, the mentally disturbed, the collaborators with the Roman occupying forces - he made it clear that all persons are children of God and heirs to the Kingdom. In the way he lived and moved, he defied all material security and committed himself, totally and unconditionally. He showed that the fulfilment of life is in giving oneself to the other. In the way he lived with his disciples he made possible participation and sharing. In his availability to all he exercised justice; in the way he became meaningful, particularly for those most suffering and afflicted, he made it clear that the Kingdom is indeed "good news to the poor". The life style of Jesus Christ was indeed a radically different way of life, based on the exercise of love (justice), sharing (participation), openness and availability, dedication and sacrifice. The power and authority embodied in his person were dedicated to love, acceptance and service.

## 2. On captivity

The life style of Jesus, his suffering and death, suggest elements of an ecclesiology. He began a movement of people for whom their way of life was the most important expression of their hope and faith in the Kingdom of Heaven. It was a way of life completely different from the Roman consumerist, populist culture, which provided "panem et circenses" for the people, but which required total submission to the secular and spiritual authority of Caesar. To be a Christian meant opting for a completely new way of life, becoming a contester, refusing Caesar as the only source of authority and acceptance of him as the only value. That is why the early Christians were branded subversive, why they had to suffer martyrdom. However, many of the values of the "Christ life", strengthened during this period of persecution, were eroded with the growing recognition of the Christian community. When the Church moved "from the tent to the palace" and "from the catacombs to the cathedral" it entered into a different phase of existence, from which is has still not completely dislodged itself. It both helped to shape many of the dominant values of European society and also felt compelled to help safeguard these values, thus renouncing the possibility of being a constant dynamic force of repentance, renewal and transformation. As a church of power it had to accept and defend values and structures that strengthen power. It became corrupted through its involvement in the use of power. Not seldom did it forget that power and authority are meant to be used for the service of others, and not for their victimization.

Of course, throughout the history of the Church there have been people who pointed to this captivity, and called the Church to repentance and renewal. Martin Luther wrote about the "Babylonian Captivity of the Church", analysing the spiritual consequences of the preoccupation of the Church with its own power and glory. But hardly ever did the church reformers analyze the captivity of the Church in structures that allow economic, social and political oppression. "Freedom" of religious conviction was and is often bought by silence in the face of social injustice. Worse, churches in many countries have come to accept a middle-class ethos and style of life as the Christian life style, to the extent that they feel Christianity itself is in danger if this style of life is called into question. In fact, the churches by and large have accepted captivity to the structures of power as their life style, thus negating discipleship and acceptance of the radically different way of Jesus Christ.

14

## 3. On repentance

"We have lost our influence because we have used it on our own behalf or on behalf of the church and not on behalf of the dispossessed, of the millions who suffer, who are hungry and are thirsty for justice." (R.F. Ceballos, Ecumenical Council of Cuba)

Repentance means looking at ourselves within the framework of interests of the total human community and acknowledging failures and shortcomings. Repentance thus has something to do with the total process of uncovering the truth. For Christians repentance implies an honest assessment of the extent to which they have been able to make the will of God, revealed in the life, death and resurrection of Christ Jesus, the frame of reference of their total existence. Repentance is never easy because it cannot remain with the past - it always has implications for our present and future conduct. It is indeed a move towards renewal and the acceptance of risk. Some churches have gone through a process of repentance and have emerged strengthened in their ministry of witnessing to the gospel. We can learn from their experiences. Thus the churches in Cuba were forced by a socialist revolution to rethink their role in society.

"Between the reformed formation we had received and the praxis of a socialist system, the Church rapidly developed its theological reflection," writes Francisco Norniella, the Moderator of the Presbyterian-Reformed Church in Cuba. "The Word of God became something nearer, more urgent, more vivid and more dramatic. The Church realized that God himself was involved in that revolutionary process which, in our case, led to the creation of a new society of greater justice for the people and of peace for society. The Gospel of 'good news for the poor,' of 'freedom for the oppressed' and 'sight for the blind' came down upon us with all its prophetical implications.

"The Church understood that that revolution which caught us up like a gigantic wave was neither the enemy nor the antithesis of the Church but, instead, a revolution that presented the Church with its greatest challenge in history, calling us to take on ourselves full responsibility as the Church of Jesus Christ.

"The Church understood, under the direct action of the Spirit, that we 'could not go up to the temple to pray' leaving at the roadside the paralytic brought there to beg, as was the case of the Church at the very beginning of its history (Acts 3: 1-10).

"This means that, on the road to the temple, the Church is interrupted by the sin of the world, by the sin of that society: a paralytic, a lame man. This man was none other than a symbol of the oppressed, exploited, despised person. And the church ran into this person when they were going up to the temple to pray. A coincidence? Or God waking up the Church to its task and responsibility? Obviously the lame man was hoping to receive something from the Church. We cannot continue our way to the temple without keeping in mind that the world of oppression, that exploited world, is waiting for the Church, hoping to receive 'something' from the Church. The apostles accepted the challenge that the oppressed person presented them and let themselves be interrupted on the way to worship. 'They had neither gold nor silver' but they had power and authority to liberate that man and restore him to his full dignity. Now they, the Church, the apostles, were able to enter the temple joyfully, _together_ with the liberated beggar.

"A church that is not relevant to the liberation of man," Norniella concludes, "has no reason to exist. Without this commitment the Church cannot reach the sublime goal of worship: worship in spirit and in truth." [1]

The experience of the Presbyterian-Reformed Church indicates very clearly that repentance is always an active process leading to renewed commitment and service.

### 4. On release

Jesus tells us that he came to release the captives, to heal the sick and to restore people to life in its fullness. His message is "good news to the poor" because it is the poor who have no security other than their hope and trust in God. It is not always easy for us to hear this message in its full liberating power because we are captivated by too much security, and are often unable to put our trust in God alone. But just as the Hebrews had to let go of their security in the wilderness and trust in God alone (Exodus 16-17), so also do we have to let go of our security, our wealth, our excess, our arms, our urge for power - of all that has captivated us - and have no security other than Christ.

Overcoming this captivity implies contesting sin embodied in the structures and the values of death and destruction that we have consolidated in mechanisms of exploitation and oppression. The invitation of Jesus to take up his cross and follow him comes to us with a new dimension: to join in contesting the principalities and powers, to be in solidarity with the community of the suffering that is struggling for a new life for all. Only in this way can we be sanctified and grow spiritually, and a new style of life emerge amidst the struggles for a more humane future.

---

1) Francisco Norniella, "Excerpts from a speech given at the 190th General Assembly of the Presbyterian Church in the United States, 1978." In Church and Society, July/October 1979, p. 111 ff.

## 5. The protest of the poor - the emerging hope

The struggle for renewal is never easy, but we need to go through it on any path towards the new. In this course there is always painful confrontation with ourselves, our attitudes and values, and with our society, its structures and institutions.

Hope is emerging in the fact that the poor, deprived and oppressed people of the world are coming of age. All over the world, especially in Third World countries, people's movements are struggling for justice and freedom from their oppression. In affluent societies, there is growing social and political awareness among people: more than ever, people are realizing that the political, economic and social structures of power which have given their countries political power and economic affluence are the same structures of power that deny and deprive of their basic rights and dignity to be human their brethren in the Third World, that abuse the ecosystem, that alienate people and turn them into mere producers of goods and services, and that deny "life abundant" in all its dimensions. The emergence of this new consciousness has given rise to many groups who are struggling in a variety of ways for the new. It is in this context that new styles of living, new values and attitudes and a new spirituality are talking shape. This new spirituality reflects the faith, hope and joy of the early Christians. It is the kind of spirituality that was born out of the oppression and struggle of the early Church.

The life situation of the oppressed people where the new is being fashioned is challenging the churches to become involved. It is a new Macedonian call to a missionary journey in reverse. As we accept this challenge, we recall the promise of Jesus that it is in losing our life that we shall find it, in dying that there will be resurrection and life eternal.

## IV. ON STRATEGY - TOWARD A NETWORK OF SOLIDARITY

The awareness present among those of us who are active in people's movements and living out alternative choices in our society is marked by an affirmation of life. One aspect of this is expressed in our desire to participate consciously, to work and serve, in solidarity with each other. This attitude of faithful hope was evident in the sharing of our experiences and in the authenticity of our involvement in many local struggles. The struggle for each is unique but, at the same time, it is born of many common experiences.

The solidarity which is growing in both the developed and underdeveloped countries is of the same flesh and blood - the workers, the peasants, the urban poor and slum dwellers, the minorities, the women and youth. They are the people who have been denied their right to a fully human life. It is the "continuum link" that bonds people all over the globe - North or South, industrial or non-industrial, consumer developed or underdeveloped. The

"thread of life" is pulled just as tight in the arena of ecological destruction as it is in the arena of economic exploitation and political oppression. Emerging forces and movements
find expression in their solidarity for political, economic and
environmental justice. However, while we affirmed the hope that
these movements embody greater strength and potential to bring
about change than all the nuclear energy of the world, we also
highlighted the isolated, localised and often marginalized and
sectarian character of many movements. Any effort to change
power structures and world policies demands planned strategies
which integrate political action with ethical values. Today,
what managers and bureaucrats plan in top level committees in one
part of the world has far-reaching implications for those who inhabit the remote corners of another part. So any movement of
those committed to change would not go very far without an international network among groups. Strategy, then, has to be re-
defined in a global perspective, within the context of the international economy and the divisions it creates between the owners
and managers of capital and the rest of humankind.

This provides the raison d'être for creating an alternative network of communication, information, education and participatory
research. The role of a world-wide counter-information service
is a vital one: it can be used as an effective vehicle of communicating to the people, in a comprehensible form and language,
facts about the decisions, policies and actions of those in power,
which have direct and often disastrous implications for the lives
of countless human beings all over the world. Such a network
would be an affirmation of their right to this knowledge, generally distorted, camouflaged or unreported by the established press
and media. Further, by publicising people's struggles all over
the world it would go a long way in forging bonds of solidarity
among the oppressed. Dialectically related to the need for alternative knowledge is participatory training and interaction with
those directly involved in struggle, so that the creation of a
new world is realized through a process which is participatory,
dynamic and humane.


V.  SOME PROPOSALS FOR ACTION

Our experience as Christians and as members of churches confirms
the fact that the institutional churches, by and large, are captives of materialism, individualism and authoritarianism. In our
theological reflection we became aware that the churches are
called to reconsider these values in the light of the values of
the Gospel and to ask to what extent their middle-class affluence
causes marginalization of those who seek social change. We asked
whether it was not necessary for the "church for the people" to
become the "church of the people", seeking ways of living in
solidarity with the poor and their struggles.

In the light of these reflections the following proposals for
action emerged.

A. **The World Council of Churches, its member churches and ecumenical partners are called:**

1. to begin a process of redefining their priorities in the line "towards a church in solidarity with the poor".

2. to support existing networks involved in people's struggles, including the formation of alliances between churches and non-church groups, and to help networks globalize the issues.

3. to develop a strategy of information/communication to inform the people in their own language, thus creating a network between the people's struggles, and to advocate better educational processes through which people can communicate and learn. In this context the CCPD Network Letter could perform a creative role.

4. to promote international networks of committed people (social scientists, economists, politicians, theologians, as well as broader church constituencies) and people's movements, to reflect together on the quality of development. This should lead to research and development of alternative scenarios arising from people's movements. In the context of this co-operation there should also be continuing examination of the conditions for a New International Economic Order and for New National Economic Orders. CCPD could play a creative role in this regard by

   - linking its Advisory Group on Economic Matters to the total CCPD network and its experiences,

   - strengthening support groups acting in solidarity with people's struggles.

5. to provide, through international linkages of the committed, opportunities for meeting together to further the sharing of experiences and development of strategies.

6. to publicize the demands of people's movements in the face of growing militarism both nationally and internationally.

7. to begin a process of institutional renewal in the World Council of Churches and its member churches, by recognizing the patterns of social discrimination that still exist in its own bodies, especially the division of labour according to sex, and inadequate representation by the Third World.

8. to achieve better participation in the life and decision-making processes of the World Council of Churches through decentralization, including the movement of many of its activities to places in the Third World where the people's struggles are.

9. finally, to encourage the spiritual process of "reconstruction of the human person" in the struggle for a "new heaven and a new earth", begun from within the old.

B. Further, churches, groups and individuals involved in people's movements are called:

1. to examine their own life styles, including that of the community or group to which they belong, and encourage their churches or organizations to give voice to the poor in their midst. In particular, churches are invited to begin a process of study on whether their institutional life styles, their salary schemes, their investment patterns and their total financial and administrative management hinder rather than help their witness to a Lord who came to announce good news to the poor. We would rejoice if churches could begin to think of possible alternatives that would allow a more authentic ministry: this could include putting their facilities at the service of the "people's movements".

2. to bring the conclusions of this consultation to the local assemblies of churches for consideration and action.

C. As participants in the new life styles consultation we close with an attempt to find ways to continue our work by establishing a process for continued communication. Thus we ask CCPD:

1. to enable a process of regional linkages by integrating representatives of people's movements/new life styles movements into the process of regional meetings.

2. to continue to act as a coordinator of these efforts through collaboration of the People's Participation and Development Education desks.

Finally, we wish to affirm our solidarity with those involved in the struggle for justice, participation and true sustainability of the earth all over the world. A true international community of the suffering, oppressed and silenced has yet to emerge, but as Christians we cannot but listen and respond to the cry for liberation, before we enter the temple joyfully.

REPORT OF THE FIRST MEETING

OF THE

CORE GROUP ON NEW LIFE STYLES


GENEVA, NOVEMBER 1977

The Core Group on New Life Styles, appointed by the Commission on the Churches' Participation in Development (CCPD), met in Geneva to share information on the present stage of national programmes on new life styles and to outline possibilities of continuing this programme of CCPD. The Core Group, with members from the Netherlands, the Federal Republic of Germany, Italy, Sweden and the USA, also heard reports of national events in Great Britain, Switzerland, Austria and Canada and of international programmes on the issue of new life styles, such as the Society for International Development (SID)/United Nations University sponsored research programme on Alternative Ways of Life. It further evaluated the reactions received to the report of the workshop in Glay (January 1977), and identified some new developments in the debate on new life styles. In the following, the Core Group shares a few points of the debate.

The Core Group also wishes to note that it felt uneasy about the term "New Life Styles" because it does not represent the full content of what is meant by new life style practitioners and because it is not used by all people striving to change the structure of their society for the betterment of their life. The Core Group has not been able to coin a new name. It feels that, whatever the name be, it should reflect the linkage between the personal way of life on the one hand and the need for systemic change on the other. It is with this reservation that the term "New Life Styles" is used in the following report.


I. THE PRESENT CLIMATE OF THE DEBATE

The climate of the debate regarding issues related to new life styles is both favourable and unfavourable.

It is favourable insofar as:

- more and more people feel that things cannot go on much longer with the recipes and aims of yesterday and today. Neither unemployment nor social peace and justice within societies, nor the problem of resources can be solved without reorientation of aims, methods and means;

- ideological concepts are no longer trusted to provide global answers. People are prepared to regard partial, temporary and incomplete attempts with greater sympathy;

- especially the idea of automatic technological progress, which will eventually create satisfactory living conditions for all, is losing ground.

It is unfavourable:

- because unemployment and permanent situations of crisis lead people to demand immediate answers: crisis management instead of long-term development has become a normal political reaction;

- because income differentials become the more unbearable as the hope of all to get more tomorrow dwindles rapidly. Reaction: a widespread clamour for the securing of what has already been achieved;

- because general resignation, stemming from the apparent impossibility of automatic progress, favours concentration on the private sphere;
- because in some countries, notably the Federal Republic of Germany, a climate of fear and a diminishing liberal atmosphere hamper open discussion. This holds true also for the climate in the established churches.

As far as the specific activities of the new life styles groups are concerned, there seems to prevail a situation where new attempts are rare, older attempts are gradually revising hopes and methods and the general public takes less notice of these things - positively and negatively - than some years ago. Coherence and a certain amount of information and exchange of experiences seem to take place in the Netherlands and Sweden and, perhaps to a lesser degree, in Switzerland.


## II. ELEMENTS OF THE DEBATE: JUSTICE, PARTICIPATION, SUSTAINABILITY

Some qualitative aspects of new life styles have lost part of their attractiveness to the public, e.g., in some countries communal living is no longer a main emphasis in the new life styles debate, while other aspects are winning public interest: here we must mention the energy debate, the issue of just distribution of income within countries, the reform of social and medical services and changes in the structures of consumption and consequently of production. There is also debate and action on how to find ways and means of more participation of people in the decision-making processes that concern their lives and their future - here both governmental and business authorities come under scrutiny.

On the other hand, there is dispute as to whether the situation does not call for a stronger state, more hierarchical structures and less free-wheeling experimenting.

The fact that in many countries vital and fundamental debates are held publicly, partly at the party and political level, may be a chance for new life styles to focus on topics such as energy, industrial structuring for the future, distribution of income and work, and the financial and ecological consequences of wasteful consumption and production patterns.

The growing awareness of people who are searching for a meaning to life may be another chance. However, we must also be aware that the temptations of sectarianism, retreat or hopelessness may be greater than the will to seek valid orientation and engage in concrete private and political action.

24

# III. SOLIDARITY

While the debate inside the industrialized countries is forced upon these countries, because of many inner contradictions that are being revealed in their social, economic and political structures, this debate has not always, and certainly not very forcefully, been linked to the question of reordering relations between rich and poor nations. Thus, we have a situation where more progressive political parties call for the reordering of basic social and individual values of their own societies, but where there is no concomitant action to redress international political and economic imbalances and to change mechanisms of domination and dependence. The New International Economic Order (NIEO) is still not accepted by the majority of industrialized countries, and voices against it come from very different quarters.

This begs the question how individual and collective efforts towards new life styles in the industrialized countries are linked to the efforts of millions of poor people in the underdeveloped world to fight for the fulfilment of basic human needs and against the violation of basic human rights.

Solidarity is required at local, national and global levels, between Christians of different social groups, between Christians and people of other political and religious convictions, and as a back-up on the part of Christians and churches to the efforts of the poor peoples and nations towards more justice.

So far, as has become clear, the new life styles movement has invited the building of all types of alliances and solidarities. This shows that the ideological content of the new life styles debate is ambiguous and that clearer reference needs to be made to the goals towards which new life styles efforts attempt to contribute. Therefore, the Core Group considered it particularly important that the future programme contribute towards the clarification of these ambiguities.


# IV. ISSUES TO BE ADDRESSED

Many activities and involvements of people all over the world can be seen as responses to a conflict between the situation in which these people live and what is now being called a "just, participatory and sustainable society".

These responses vary between cultures, between socio-economic systems, between classes.

New life styles, too, are such a response which can be found in the rich, industrialized countries, mainly reflected upon and practised by middle-class people. There is a need to link this attempt with those emanating from other contexts and to confront it with these other responses so that it can truly be said that new life styles contribute to the realization of a society in which the right of the poor is put first and foremost in personal life and societal structures.

In this context, efforts at new life styles could be considered as the creation within present-day society of free spaces where the values of a just, participatory and sustainable society begin to be realized. They are the anticipation of a more humane and more just society, the anticipation of things to come, and in faith they are the anticipation of the Kingdom. In a society where maximization of profit and exploitation of humans by humans are still the rule, efforts at new life styles are like "liberated zones," to be continuously widened and extended, like a permanent invitation to the public at large to change their ways of looking at themselves, others and nature, side by side with, and participating in, the larger systemic changes taking place in society.

The fact that new life styles arise in a specific context (that of middle-class people in the industrialized world) gives rise to a number of questions:

- Efforts at new life styles are motivated by a number of urgent questions related to conflicts within societies (unemployment, alienation), between societies (rich/poor countries, food situation, armament and militarism) and between generations (ecological issues). Do these efforts properly perceive these problems? And, if so, is their analysis of their causes and possible solutions an adequate one?

- Do the solutions put forward or supported by new life styles efforts imply proper involvement in the struggle for the necessary changes in the socio-economic system, or do they in fact work against other forces that work towards such changes? Are new life styles efforts in danger of being coopted by forces that effectively sustain present systems or slow down the pace of change?

It is our conviction that real changes towards a just, participatory and sustainable society will come through the inner strength of the poor who, in their struggle for mere survival or in their attempts to overcome the structures of domination as the root cause of their oppression, create the basis for the future society. Efforts at new life styles should thus be in solidarity with the struggle of the poor. Their priorities should be set by the poor and they should be inserted into the strategy for change which the poor themselves have adopted. This might be the only way to avoid the cooptation of new life styles efforts by forces wanting to maintain or simply re-arrange the system of oppression.

In many practical cases, new life styles efforts can be seen as directly supporting the struggles of the poor, e.g., where they work with migrant labourers in West European countries, promote the sale of Third World products, or work towards emancipation of and participation by marginal groups and classes in society. In other cases, it is not so clear that there is a complete convergence of insights and interests. By way of illustration we list some examples related to the criteria of a just, partici-

26

patory and sustainable society.

Where new life style efforts support the implementation of a new international economic order, they encounter the dilemma that the _just_ claim by the Third World for better terms of trade would lead to increased unemployment in Western societies, which might imply popular reaction there against such proposals.

In acting against nuclear energy, new life styles efforts are motivated by the notion of _sustainability_. However, many in the Third World would say that they cannot do without that source of energy. And, in addition to that, it may be felt that the activism in the industrialized countries against nuclear energy compared with the lack of action against the arms industry reflects wrong priorities.

What should be done so that new life styles efforts become real alternatives and not escapist solutions? It is the responsibility of larger bodies (like the press) or institutions like the churches to present and encourage these efforts (if understood in the sense described above) as concrete attempts to take part in the struggle for a new society and to see to it that what is an anticipation by some is critically followed by the rest of society.

Movements like the women's liberation movement can be seen as attempts to erase one feature of domination that stands in the way of _participation_. But this issue is seen differently in different contexts. In the Third World the priority of systemic change is not always accompanied by a process of liberation in the personal sphere where traditional, culturally-determined patterns remain.

This small list of examples should be refined by the Core Group in collaboration with others, notably representatives from the Third World.

CONSULTATION ON NEW LIFE STYLES

GLAY, FRANCE

JANUARY 31 - FEBRUARY 5, 1977

# I. THEOLOGICAL REFLECTIONS IN THE CONTEXT OF THE SEARCH FOR NEW LIFE STYLES

## 1. Christians and the Search for New Life Styles

Throughout the affluent world the emergence of groups of people searching for new life styles can be observed.  Reacting against prevailing patterns of behaviour, stereotyped attitudes and in-dividualistic values, these groups are trying to open up ways to a renewed life.  In this process Christians participate with non-Christians, and such involvement leads some of us to raise ques-tions concerning our faith and our witness in society.  Although in most cases our participation is not motivated by theological thinking, we feel we cannot avoid discussing such questions.

For example, in the developed world we are increasingly becoming aware of ecological problems and are trying to develop respon-sible attitudes and behaviour vis-à-vis nature and available resources.  What we are after is a new life style, in which past mistakes are corrected.  We form groups and associations aiming at a more harmonious relationship between human beings and en-vironment, developing our action through campaigns and by other methods, oriented towards awareness-building on these problems. For us, nature is not opposed to human life, but is its necessary context.  To continue to abuse nature or to destroy it is to damage what is human.  Some of us involved in this type of ac-tion, which manifests a new life style vis-à-vis nature, are in effect posing theological questions: How to understand creation through which the redemptive work of God is being accomplished? How to be responsible in our relationship with nature, also reflecting our faithfulness to God who is Creator and Redeemer? What corrections are needed in theologies that see nature only as a reservoir of raw materials at the disposal of human beings, and not as a gift of God to human beings of all ages?  These and similar questions are posed in the context of the search for the new, of renewal of human life, of attempts to express "a new life style".

We are also becoming aware of the great disparities between life in developed and underdeveloped countries.  We feel uneasy about the possibility and degree of consumption of the rich, which is in contrast with the scarcity and suffering of the poor majority of the world's population.  We think it necessary to curb con-sumption in affluent countries and call the attention of their peoples to this problem, inviting them "to live more simply in order that others may simply live".  We Christians concerned about a new life style feel this is a way to express - at least in part - our responsibility towards the poor of this world. Why accumulate the superfluous and waste unnecessarily while so many others are struggling merely to survive?  For some of us, giving full expression to this responsibility involves going further and making a necessary complementary step: to share with those in need whatever results from our resolve to curb consump-tion.  This may be an expression of Christian charity, but it is also a witness of the concern for those in need, especially in the Third World.  Simplicity and solidarity go hand in hand in

31

this case. In this context the teachings of the Epistle of James, calling believers in Jesus Christ to oneness, become a challenge in our present world. Christian fellowship is not limited to those who live around us; those of us practising this life style say that it has to reach the least of the poor, among whom Jesus Christ expects manifestation of our love and care (Matt. 25:31-46).

Many, if not all, of us are convinced that, in fellowship with other peoples, we must also try to advance social justice in the world. The search for new life styles cannot be separated from community life. We are concerned, for example, with the situation of migrant workers in affluent countries, as well as with social, economic and political structures which allow some to take advantage of the work of many. We are involved in social mobilization, in conscientization efforts, in political struggles... Some of us are motivated by ideologies which claim to achieve equity and a more human society. As Christians we are becoming involved in such efforts as ways of witnessing to a life lived in the expectation of the "Kingdom of God", of a world of justice and freedom. We believe that our participation in these movements is in opposition to the way of life which creates "massification" and indifference about social, economic and political matters. For us, to live in this way, militating for justice, in the expectation of the Kingdom, is to give expression to what St. Paul wrote: "Adapt yourselves no longer to the pattern of this present world, but let your minds be remade and your whole nature thus transformed. Then you will be able to discern the will of God, and to know what is good, acceptable, and perfect" (Rom. 12:2). Our life style is perhaps not entirely new, but we try to innovate, to re-create, to open new avenues and build new channels of human relationships in society. For us, this is related to the Kingdom for whose coming we pray. So prayer for us is an expression of our deep feelings and expectations.

We also denounce the growing gap between developed and underdeveloped people, and we seek a more equitable world. Our claim is for "another development", to correct prevailing patterns of economic growth. We emphasize the need for technology which can be appropriated by and for everybody. We would give warning of the unpredictable damaging consequences of the expanding use of nuclear energy for future generations of humanity. Through these lines of action we are searching for a new life style corresponding to the "New International Economic Order", which implies changes not only at the international level but in national structures as well. Again, as Christians involved in the practice of this life style, we ask for simpler living and for solidarity with the poor and the victims of injustice. In this context, we relate the vision of the new world order to the search for a new society. Although we realize their limitations, we strive for change as a form of participation in the mission of the Church, which we understand not only as proclamation, but also as involvement in the cause of justice and peace among nations. We believe that, from a theological perspective, it is necessary to rediscuss the problem posed by the contradiction between the powers of the world and the authority of Jesus Christ. We are not trying to justify our action through this kind of reflection, but to understand how we should work at this level of human life.

As an implication of the commitments indicated above, we feel compelled to develop and strengthen different types of community life in order to counter prevailing patterns of individualistic existence which create alienation, lack of personal communication with others and loss of the sense of community. This movement is visible particularly among the younger generation: it is an affirmation of collective and communitarian values, as well as an existential active search for more appropriate social structures for human beings. As Christians involved in such processes we ask ourselves about the relationship of these forms of living together with the meaning of fellowship (koinonia) for the people of God. Instead of thinking in terms of "social order" we think rather in terms of how the Holy Spirit is uniting people, how He is at work renewing our existence through this style of life and creating conditions for potential changes in society. Most of these expressions of living together have service in society as a purpose, which poses the question again to us about the relation between community and service (koinonia and diakonia) as a manifestation of the fruits of the Holy Spirit (Gal. 5:22-23).

Many of us involved in new life styles movements have made fundamental and even radical decisions. Some of us have been motivated by the others' suffering, because of our feelings of social responsibility. In the midst of these situations we have experienced "the love of Christ which leaves us no choice" (II Cor. 5:14), which has helped us to reorient our ways of living, trying to achieve a more meaningful personal and collective human existence. In this context, the different involvements in the search for new life styles may very well be expressions - almost signs - of the continual renewal of all things by Jesus Christ through his Holy Spirit.


2.  Some Points of Departure

Having sketched the main aspects of the context in which the search for new life styles takes shape today, we indicate in the following some points of departure for further theological reflection. Instead of making a systematic presentation, without any claim to comprehensiveness we propose three possible lines of thought in an endeavour to relate traditional theological discourse to the present-day life style discussion and vice versa. The first section on "Co-workers of God" has its context in the tradition of the Reformation, while the two sections on "The Church and the Cosmos" and on "The Sacrament of the Poor" are rooted in the tradition of eastern orthodox theology.


a)  Co-workers of God

The search for a new life style takes place in the context of the apparently irredeemable, world-wide self-destruction of mankind. The powerful few exploit the vast masses of the powerless, reducing them to a state of extreme poverty, even delivering them to certain death, and in doing so they destroy the very basis of life itself. This historical setting is experienced by many as a combination of destructive trends which converge in a process that leads irreversibly towards a fatal destiny.

The growing momentum of the search for new life styles cannot be removed from this context. It reveals the conviction that new life is possible in spite of and "from beyond" the apparent hopelessness of the situation. Irrespective of its different, specific motivations and its different expressions in different settings, this search - in all its pluralistic manifestations - has a common thrust: it affirms the principle of hope, and thus negates the power of fatalistic necessity.

The fact that many individuals and groups searching for new life styles live outside or on the fringe of the institutional church poses a serious challenge to all those who profess to be servants of the Gospel. Is it not the Church which claims to live by the promise "Behold, I make all things new"? (Rev. 21:5). Should the manifestation of hope in the face of hopelessness not be the central event which continuously regenerates the life of the Church as a genuine demonstration of eschatological existence? In other words, is not the task of the Church, her very raison d'être, to affirm a life born of the promise of the new in the midst of the threats of the time? Is not the Church called to manifest the certain trust that the Lord meets us in the dark future, a trust which does not remove the darkness but which deprives it of its power? And is it not in a life of such hope that the power of the Gospel removes resignation and opens our eyes so that we may discover the manifold signs through which the promised new life announces itself as a foretaste of the coming of the Kingdom?

The numerous endeavours in search of a new life style reveal an affinity with an eschatological understanding of the Kingdom of God in history. As an affirmation of hope they experience the tension between the "not yet" and the "already amongst you", a tension which the Church herself has often tried to maintain. Can we discern, in the search for new life styles and its implicit trust that new life is possible, that God is still with his creation? And, if so, how does this affect the witness of the Church? Does all this remain peripheral or does the Church perceive it as a call to repentance?

The significance of the search for the new becomes even clearer if we consider another aspect of its affinity with the biblical witness. This search calls into question certain basic assumptions of the form of scientific/technological development which dominates our lives. It rejects, fairly explicitly, the notion that nature is merely a reservoir of resources for our unrestricted use. In groping for a new life style we are undergirded in one way or another by the conviction that we must discover and practise forms of personal conduct which are oriented towards the maintenance of life on this planet and informed by the desire for just distribution of our limited resources. Central to the affirmation of these aims is the acceptance of finitude, the acceptance of the limits to our existence. But such acceptance strikes at the very heart of the development which we

practise at present, for our present form of development is by
its very nature the negation of finitude. We begin to understand it ever more clearly as the culmination of the Promethean
revolution which - determined to destroy the limitations of
creatureliness - destroys creation itself.

The Church should have no problem in understanding the significance of such affirmations since these reflect essential biblical
views. The creation story projects a vision of man as the co-
creator, as the one who, on behalf of God, is to tend creation.
The task of "having dominion over them" is given to man who has
not yet partaken of the fruit, that is, to man who - together
and in harmony with all of creation - exists in "natural" finitude: finitude understood not as a prison but rather as the
realm in which the fullness of life unfolds. Throughout the biblical witness the vision of the reconciliation of human beings
with each other and with all of creation occupies a central
place. It shines forth in the messianic prophesies (Is. 11:1-10),
it is taken up in the beatitudes in which the land is promised
to the meek. To St. Paul (Rom. 8) the promise of the new life
issues in the conviction that in Christ all of creation will receive justice through the gift of justification (our reinstate-
ment into the role of co-creator?) to us. Does this not imply
that the exploitation of nature and of man stem from the same
root and that social justice cannot be achieved without justice
for all creation?

Seen in this context, our continued exploitation of our fellow-
creatures is a practical denial of our Easter faith, irrespective
of what we profess with our lips. By the same token, the longing
for other modes of living may in its depth be understood as the
yearning for an Easterly existence.

b) The Church and the Cosmos

Between the resurrection of Christ and the fulfilment of the
Kingdom of God, is the Church. The Church since Whit Sunday,
animated by the action of the Holy Spirit, has been the place of
personal encounter between God and human beings. Her consti-
tutive element is the eucharist. Each Christian, through the
eucharist, is in communion with other members of this community
and also with a Trinitarian God. It is the birth of cosmos like
a body of Glory; it is the rebirth of humanity assumed and re-
deemed by Christ. The Church through her liturgical life is the
divine human place, where the universal body of the new human
being is slowly created. The entire creation suffers the pains
of childbirth until the moment of its regeneration (Rom. 8:20-22).
The mysteries of the Church, that is to say, the different
aspects of the life of the ecclesial community, are the centre
and the sense of cosmic life. Things are assumed and sanctified
by the prayers and blessings of the Church. In every civilization we see two tendencies: the wish to return to Paradise,
through feast, art and leisure, where human beings freely admire
nature; and work as humanization of the world. Here, human
beings are called upon to collaborate with God for the salvation
of the universe. In the knowledge of nature and in its transformation, it is up to us to live a cosmis eucharist. "That

which is yours and which comes from you, we offer it to you, all and for all" (Liturgy St. John Chrysostomos).

c) The Sacrament of the Poor (Matt. 25:31-46)

Personal existence in the ecclesial community is an existence of communion with other persons, according to the image of the Trinitarian God, whose essence is love. "That is the distinction between the children of God and the children of the devil: no one who does not do right is God's child, nor is anyone who does not love his brother" (I John 3:10). We have to bear in mind the Last Judgement. Christ tells the just ones: "You have my Father's blessing; come, enter and possess the kingdom that has been ready for you since the world was made. For when I was hungry, you gave me food; when thirsty, you gave me drink; when I was a stranger you took me into your home, when naked you clothed me; when I was ill you came to my help, when in prison you visited me" (Matt. 25:34-36). It was John Chrysostomos who spoke in relation to this text about "the sacrament of the brother", and especially of "the least" among the brothers, that is, the poor. Chrysostomos strove for the freedom of spirit and the rights of the poorest of Constantinople confronted with the imperial power, paying for that with martyrdom. Chrysostomos emphasized that Christ is the other, and that the sacrament of the eucharist must be at the service of justice, that is, like an oblation, which is not an expression merely of piety but of sharing in order to achieve a better social life.

The sharing of goods as was done in the Church of Jerusalem has remained throughout the history of Christianity the inductive image, not of an economic system that would resolve all problems (which has never been the case), but of the victory of human will over egoism and greed, in order to live "unanimously" in love.

Many Fathers of the Church underlined the relative character of private property and strongly criticized the heritage of the means of production. They also showed that natural resources belong to God and that human beings should only make use of them for the good of all. Simultaneously they rehabilitated human work, which was considered servile in the Greco-Roman civilization. The example is given by St. Paul in making tents. The Fathers saw in human work the cosmic responsibility of the human person and the expression of solidarity through which communion is manifested.

When Constantinian conformism turned Christian parishes into groups of indifferent people, the possibilities of expressing love (agape) and living fellowship decreased. It was at that time that monastic communities appeared. They aimed at giving witness of the apostolic love, and bringing back to life, in a new historical context, the example of the first Church of Jerusalem. Monasteries, always open to people and where all monks had to work (as is still the case in Eastern churches), were a demonstration of the fact that rejection of oneself demands the rejection of riches.

The movements for evangelical poverty that shook societies in the late Middle Ages and at the beginning of modern times were echoes of the teachings of St. John Chrysostomos. These movements, severely repressed, were an expression of one of the most disastrous schisms in the history of Christianity: the schism between the sacrament of the altar and the sacrament of the poor. The Church has preserved the mystery and mystique of the Risen Lord, but many Christians have very often demonstrated a lack of sensitivity to the crucified Christ of history among the poorest, especially during and after the Industrial Revolution (many factors in Church history led to this situation: the decline of monasticism, the development of individualistic piety, without much ability to provoke creative ethics, and so on).

The evolution of the functions of deacons is illustrative of such distortions: in the Early Church the deacon gave the eucharist the whole of its social dimension: acting on behalf of the bishop, he was the person responsible for the social work of the church to be performed as a sacrament. However, through the ages, the ministry of the deacon has <u>de facto</u> disappeared in the West, and has become merely liturgical in the East. When separated from the eucharist - by which alone the sacrament of the poor can be revitalized - those who were able to understand and practise the sacrament of the poor have oriented their hopes to the violence of utopias, towards the passionate expectation of a "millinarian Kingdom", which could be realized through some kind of liberating catastrophe. Here we face the origins of modern socialism.

There is no guide to the action of Christians other than active, creative, stubborn love, always ready to begin to move again, and animated by the vision of the whole person as a co-worker of God.


## 3.   The Churches and the Search for New Life Styles

There is a process of challenge between Christians and churches participating in the search for new life styles. It would be unfortunate if the opportunity for fruitful dialogue were lost, because of either party's refusal to discuss these problems with the other; for example, the churches request participants in different groups striving for new life styles to reflect upon how their concern is related to Christian faith, to the repentance of sins, to conversion and salvation, to the redemptive work of God, and so on. Churches have every right to remind those involved in this active research not to lose, but rather to improve, their understanding of their Christian contribution to society and to the Church.

In the same way, Christians involved in these processes have every right to challenge the prevailing life style in many churches, which to many has become a "weekend parenthesis" or, to others, a reflection of the existence of enclaves in which a formalistic piety is exercised and which is characterized by an undeniable trend to comfortable "embourgeoisement". Because of this, for many Christians who search for new life styles, church life is a synonym for conformism, that is, lack of creativity

37

and freedom. But what does a "new life style" mean to the churches? To be faithful to Jesus Christ is to be open to the renewal that the Holy Spirit brings about within the people of God.

The churches, then, in one way or another have to answer such questions as: How do different manifestations of the search for new life styles affect the life of the Christian congregation? How do we express a new life style in the missionary work of the Church? What is the relationship between new ways of living and liturgical forms in the life of the Church? In what ways can church structures be open to the challenges posed by the search for new life styles? In what ways do power structures within the churches manifest people's real participation in decision-making processes? How can we avoid a situation in which, while the life style of committed believers in Jesus Christ is changing, the institutional life styles of the churches continue to remain more or less the same? How can churches become appropriate groups or fellowships for people's search for new life styles? How do we understand the concept of stewardship in our time?

We feel that consideration of some of these questions by churches immediately following this meeting would be helpful.

## II. LIVING TOGETHER AND NEW LIFE STYLES

Although the task of the group was to take up and discuss the
issue of community life, and report its observations and conclusions, the proliferation of thoughts on the subject led the
members to identify the following six major areas that they considered important and to present their ideas in written form
only on these areas.

1. Motivations for living together
2. Expectations, aims and purposes of community life
3. Examples of forms of community
4. Criteria for meaningful community
5. Hindrances to community
6. Sexuality and life styles

The reports were drafted by different members of the group who
tried to incorporate the thinking of the group, but they clearly
reflect a personal bias. Thus, this report is much like the
Bible in that it has many different authors all guided by the
same Spirit.

Discussion began with narration of personal experiences in community living and the concerns that these evoked. This helped
identification of the major topics reported. However, many
other equally important issues were discussed which the group
was unfortunately unable to record. The following is a brief
outline of these other issues:

- Community life in the Third World; the problem of industrialization; what "the North" has to offer the Third World countries
  and vice versa, with respect to community life.

- Analysis of a model of a new society with community at the
  centre, and its role in systemic change.

- The church as a mediating force in changing society; the role
  of the pastor in living a new life style.

- The striving to make utopia real through gestures or images
  which foresee the future. The prophetic role of theology.

- Romanticism and nostalgia in the search for community. The
  call to return home. The call to freedom.

- The apparent need for charismatic leaders in communities.

- Differences in communities and concern for new life styles in
  different cultures and different countries.

As a result of all the discussions a final but essential contribution was added, which is a list of proposals for further steps
to be taken by CCPD on the issue of alternative life styles and
community life.

## 1. Motivations for Living Together

Discussion on the different reports of living together heard by the group led to the realization that a series of motivations must be taken into account.

### A. Nature

There is acute awareness of waste and bad use of nature which can be described as follows:

- dying out of nature
- waste of natural resources, and especially of energy
- lack of knowledge of the ecosystem
- inappropriate or dangerous interventions in the ecosystem
- misuse of some important energy resources
- the daily working life is placed in a very artificial context, thus widening the gap between the daily working life, with the relationships it creates, and natural conditions of life.

### B. The human being

Another series of motivations emerges from the knowledge that the human being and the human group are also dying out. On this point people are acutely aware of the risks being taken, and some countries are facing a problem to which they have given considerable thought.

The following were noted:

- the fact that people are becoming more anonymous and isolated;
- the consequences of "massification" which proffers models in the realms of work, personal relationships, leisure and social security which are too abstract, anonymous and impersonal;
- the impossibility of practising some styles of life because:

  a) some functions always belong to the family, but the family has neither time, place, economic means nor freedom to perform them;

  b) the human functions of any social group are neglected by cultural models which place more importance on production than on the nurture of relationships, and do not guarantee either sufficient jobs or satisfying work on material, spiritual, symbolic or human levels.

One basic motivation is thus to be found at the level of emotional isolation. People, groups, the nuclear family, etc., remain too isolated and suffer from this cruel anonymity.

### C. Things

There is growing awareness of the banality and futility of many of the objects used by people. This seems to be due to several factors, especially:

40

- the accelerated multiplicity of objects in daily life;
- advertising which gives goods false and provisional meanings;
- continuous promotion of consumerism, encouragement of waste, collection of useless objects leading to apathy towards things (and situations) and making the object system more remote from objective social use;
- narrowing of the definition of a human produce - only the material production of people is taken into account, to the exclusion of their spiritual, symbolic and relational production.

Vision of the world - anxieties and attempted solutions: This more or less unconscious vision can be summed up in the dying out of nature, the human being and the meaning of things. People therefore have cause to be anxious. They react by attempting solutions such as:

- rules for economizing and better use of human resources (ecological, energetic, objects, etc.);
- the search for some styles of life inspired by the past but adapted to the present (move from a family with blood ties to an open family with relationships based on both blood ties and friendship);
- the tightening of relationships among people who live in the same neighbourhood or buildings or who have face-to-face relationships, or share common goods or goals;
- the conscientization of wider sections of populations to make them aware of the problems and the chances of success of some of the sólutions already tried out.

Towards a clearer vision of the New Community: Beyond these isolated approaches, a more radical solution is emerging in the search for a new society and a new culture which might inspire an integrated vision of what is being done or should be endeavoured and what is capable of integrating the world, things and the human group. This basic vision is attained by several ideal projects which all try to respond to the variables already mentioned. They are put forward as examples which may be adopted by an ever-growing number of people.

The following questions, however, must be raised:

1. In what countries or social classes are conditions such that anxiety would lead people to implement such projects?
2. To what extent can these new visions become models accepted and practised by whole populations and not small groups?

## 2. Expectations, Aims and Purposes of Community Life

The deficiencies of prevailing patterns in the "private" sphere
of life largely determine the expectations, aims and purposes
of a wide variety of forms of community living and of "living
together".  It is expected and hoped:

a)   that a unit larger than the so-called "nuclear family" will
     be able to live with less expenditure on the paraphernalia
     of modern life, such as cars, household machines, one-purpose
     rooms, energy; that is, that a desired standard of living
     will be achieved with less waste of money, time and effort.

b)   that such a unit, whatever its size and organizational
     stringency, will increase the freedom of time for all mem-
     bers, and allow its flexible use for whatever individual
     members wish or need to do.  This is hoped and expected
     particularly with regard to female members of such a group:
     they can be enabled better and more easily to live a full
     life, according to their wishes and the tasks to be fulfilled
     at a given time and stage of life, without ruining their
     health and nerves by combining work in and for the family
     with other interests and obligations.

c)   that it will be possible in such a larger unit to re-
     emphasize the familial roles and possibilities of the male
     members: to partake more intensely in important aspects of
     so-called "private life" - the household and upbringing of
     children; to make themselves more useful by pragmatically
     and systematically participating in household work according
     to their abilities and the needs of the moment, and not
     according to some standardized idea of male or female types
     of work; they may also more easily realize, for instance,
     the wish to change professions than would otherwise be
     possible.

d)   that larger units - whatever the priorities in the social,
     political and religious fields may be - may also create an
     atmosphere of mutual encouragement in attempts to pursue new
     aims and give greater value to things which are not in the
     centre of prevailing life styles: for instance, the wish to
     become free of the pressures of consumerism, of buying things
     for their alleged prestige value, of the wasteful habits of
     a throwaway economy.

e)   that such larger units will aim to free their adult members
     from two evils: the frequent loneliness of living as a single
     person and the often nerve-racking experience of living in a
     tightly closed marriage and nuclear family; that it will also
     be helpful in preventing some of the resulting damage to
     children typical of today's one or two children families:
     their lack of contact with other children and adults which
     whom  they can have close and steady emotional contacts.

f)   that the aims and expectations of those groups will not
     exclude and reject the institution of marriage as such: the
     aim in most cases will not be to replace the institution of
     marriage and of the nuclear family but to open up these

units and to bridge the gap between the isolated private family sphere and the big, anonymous social agencies and institutions, so that not all the needs of the individual regarding personal relationships, friendships, acceptance, understanding, etc., need to be met exclusively by one partner.

g) that some of the richness in functions, in emotional fulfil- ment, in the ways, means and forms of contacts and relations of persons to each other, which the larger family of pre- industrial societies and the more closely-knit neighbourhoods of former times had, will be reintroduced into the sphere of the family, and "private life" in general; that a more humane, less functionalized, less anonymous, less one-sided form of "living together" will be recreated.

h) that the larger family and other forms of living together will be attempts to repersonalize important group relation- ships and functions: to create room for manoeuvring between the small cells of the nuclear family and the depersonalized and anonymous superstructures of business, of organizations of all sorts, of state agencies, etc., which supposedly exist for the purpose of our social and individual welfare.

i) that these personalized units will be much better able than isolated nuclear families and single persons to cope with the foreseeable challenges of the near future: the challenge of altering the material conditions of life; the challenge of changing patterns of production and consumption; the challenge of re-assessing personal and social values with regard to what should be given priority; the challenge of giving high priority to values like tenderness, intensive and caring relationships to the things we live off and with; a renewed sense of the historical dimensions of each human being's life, of the chances and dignity and worth of each stage and age in life; that they will aim at a renewed sense of the importance and dignity of elementary human emotions and needs, of the times for sorrow and for joy, of the need to be alone and the need to share with others.

j) above all, that the things that really concern us will be realized more fully and within the range of our own personal experience, of our own possibilities of reacting creatively to the challenges of the day and the hour.

Most of these aims and hopes have been fundamental to all people at all times in history. Efforts are being made to repair  some of the serious deformations which have happened to us (created by us) in the course of secularization, of segregation of spheres of life which belong together, and of one-sided dominance of economic thinking and forces in the shaping of our day-by-day social, public and private life.

43

3. Examples of Forms of Community

A. Communes - formed by single people, couples, families and different generations: the reasons for living together, in addition to those mentioned under 1. and 2. (motivations, expectations), may be social, political, religious, economic, etc.

a) Communes whose members work outside but live together, acting in an organized way about public issues.

b) Communities whose members work together but do not live together, e.g.
- collectives for people who require legal advice
- groups of doctors working together
- agricultural cooperatives
- groups of journalists
- cooperatives for film production
- anti-apartheid movements; Amnesty International groups, etc.

Some of these groups work on the basis of equality (equal rights, responsibilities and salaries, etc.) and find work more satisfying as a result.

c) Communes whose members live and work together, e.g.
- agricultural communes for agricultural production and handicrafts for their own consumption or use and for sale to others; for the re-use of abandoned buildings and fields;
- therapeutic communes for drug addicts, etc.;
- working communes for the joint running of a business, such as a restaurant or small industry.

B. Family: The family will remain as the main form of life together but its make-up may change, e.g.,
- larger families, where different generations and also per-haps the handicapped live together, and where the old people continue to be seen as useful;
- several families living closer together and thus more open, more mutually responsible and more caring towards each other than they could be in a flat, street or village;
- new rules and relationships among the members of the family (see motivations and expectations);
- a couple, married or unmarried, living together on the basis of equality, thus enabling each person to be free and to be by himself/herself when desired;
- cooperative of families (e.g., in the Third World) for common production, marketing and purchasing of machines, etc.

44

## 4. Criteria for Meaningful Community

Many things make a community meaningful and operational, but the following emerge as essential.

a)  **A common interest**: The initial common bond within a community can be a common political or religious ideology, common work or commitment, or a family relationship.

b)  **A clear structure**: The structure may range from a loose organization, as in a neighbourhood community or reflection group, to a more rigid organization, as in a large commune. Though the correct amount of organization cannot be fixed in advance, the two extremes of "do-your-own-thing" and institutionalization invariably lead to dissolution of the community. An important aspect of the structure is a form of leadership that is acceptable to all.

c)  **A process of decision-making**: Since people living together cannot always agree, there is need for some way of dealing with both communal problems and interpersonal conflicts. In established communities, there is usually a weekly or monthly house meeting. The degree of friendship between members of a community determines the degree of formality of the process of decision-making.

With specific respect to residential communities or communes, these further functional criteria emerge:

d)  **Norms, rules and discipline**: In the case of communes, rules are necessary for practical reasons, for example, concerning eating, cleaning, maintenance, noise, use of communal possessions, etc. In addition, social norms must be respected, for example, norms regarding the private ownership of property, sexual roles and sexuality, private life, the raising of children. If problems arise in these areas, rules may have to replace the norms. To ensure the functioning of a commune, discipline and respect for democratic decisions are essential.

e)  **Privacy**: Because rules tend to restrict private life, the need for privacy always emerges. Conscious decision is therefore often necessary to ensure privacy. In this connection, it should be noted that families often find greater privacy in communal living because children have more choice of people to be with.

f)  **Adequate economic base**: A group cannot survive on ideals; material needs must be satisfied. That is not to say the more money the better, but an adequate income is necessary to allow the commune to function; the pooling of resources often makes it possible for members of a group to work fewer hours and earn less money and still be able to live adequately.

## 5. Hindrances to Community

The following is only a first effort to enumerate some of the hindrances to meaningful community life. It suffers from the haste in which it was written under the pressure of producing something within the context of a workshop. Even more significantly, it suffers from the fact that it was written by one whose life is limited to the experiences of nuclear family life in the USA plus just under four years of communal life.

"Hindrances" are seen here as those factors which inhibit persons from finding ways of life together which are in harmony with Christian principles. There is no attempt to spell out the criteria of what truly Christian modes of living together might be (that is an important task which still remains to be done), but the following list is offered with that consciousness.

What are some of the hindrances?

- valuing things more than each other;
- valuing things more than nature;
- valuing things more than one's self;
- sexism, including the denial of our androgynous nature;
- classism;
- racism;
- acting as if stereotypes were real, that is, treating each other as members of categories, and not finding the time or the processes to get to know each other as persons;
- hopelessness, or a lack of compelling visions, such as that of a "Just, Participatory and Sustainable Society";
- fear that emerging experiments in community living represent a threat to family life;
- industrialization:
  a) Industrialization depends on persons being unable to supply their needs except through the use of money.
  b) Centralized production requires both physical and emotional separation of home life and work life.
  c) Forced mobility results in a continuing process of breaking up meaningful community.
  d) People are treated like expendable commodities.
  e) Actions are based on the illusion that natural resources are inexhaustible or that technology will somehow come up with substitutes.
  f) Industrialization is dependent on people being taught to compete rather than to cooperate - thus we are unskilled at loving whilst highly skilled at fighting.
- mythologies of "expertise": the compartmentalization of skills causes us to discount our ability to be self-reliant;
- urbanization;

- architecture which tends to isolate persons from each other and from a sense of being connected with the earth. The utilitarian aspects of our existence are devalued and further mystified. For example, elaborate measures are taken to keep pipes, wires and other mechanical devices out of sight. Thus we lose touch with what is really required to support our styles of life;

- the notion that one's personal power is realized through domination of others: thus both self and others are devalued;

- a tradition which views violence as the ultimate solution to problems;

- the isolation of middle and upper class people from even having to see the misery of the poor;

- the notion that alternative forms of community are new and thus to be feared, whilst in reality much of what is sought in these communities represents a return to the richness of the extended families of the past;

- a tendency, on the other hand, to romanticize the past and wish to repeat it exactly which is a hindrance to building workable community for the present;

- lack of networks of support and communication between new life style pioneers;

- a lack of endorsement of experimentation by respected institutions, such as the church.


6. Sexuality and Life Styles

Sexuality is an integral but usually undiscussed and undiscussable part of our community experience and our spirituality. Any attempt to develop an analysis of life together demands a much more adventurous and direct analysis of loving relationships within community as well as physical lust and its appropriate and inappropriate place. Such relationships and lustfulness can contribute to sexual harmony and/or disharmony.

With this in mind, a series of questions arises, some appropriate for new life styles situations in general, some more fitting for communitarian situations. For example: Can we sanction what seem to be genuinely loving relationships outside of marriage? What problems and questions do such relationships raise? In what ways can forms of "living together" be affected by patterns of sexual relationships which exist outside of the married couple? How should the responsibility for children be conceived where such patterns exist?

# III. SYSTEMIC CHANGES AND NEW LIFE STYLES

## Introduction

Oh Lord, we hear the sighs of your creation.
As we continue to rape the earth,
Our heart is full of fear.
We destroy the splendour and the source of life,
And yet, we benefit from it.

Oh Lord, we hear the groaning of all mankind.
Does not our heart burn with compassion
For that broken humanity,
Our brothers and sisters
In the ghettos of New York,
In the slums of Calcutta.
Our very existence is put to shame,
And yet, we live with it.

Oh Lord, we see the writing on the wall,
We gaze at the growing sophistication
Of the mechanisms of exploitation,
We understand that the system works in our favour,
We cultivate misery
And the power to destroy.
Are we not consumed by anger,
Are we not dazed with despair
Because we are powerless, because we cannot move?

And yet, that very system
Provides our daily bread
And our daily comfort,
And so we cannot move
Because we do not wish to move.

Oh Lord, to you we lift our outspread hands,
Our heart is not ready to care,
Our hands are not ready to share,
Every day we hurt those we love,
We inflict pain on them who are closest to our hearts,
Again and again we do not have the courage to take a position
Because we fail to discern the signs of your presence in people,
Because we fail to discern the signs of your presence in all
of your creation.

We do not know how to live in the promise;
We have closed our heart to the cloud of saints,
The host of witnesses that have tried
To live in the image
Of our Brother Jesus.
We are afraid to take the way of the cross,
We are afraid of death,
We are proud,
We are broken.

And yet, we long to be your people, Lord.
As we struggle in the wilderness
Bind us together in a covenant
Turned towards one another
And towards you.

Lord, fill us with your spirit,
Let your power be present
In our weakness.

Help us to oppose the misuse of your creation,
Help us to fight those structures
Which break the poor
And shame the rich.

Lord, help us to be
Where Jesus was,
With the oppressed,
With the captives,
With the poor,
He who became nothing for our sake.

Help us to move,
To take a position,
To accept the consequence.

Oh Lord,
We long to be made whole,
We long to be made new,
One people,
One humanity.
We long to live together
In the splendour of the risen Christ.

Amen.


## 1.  The Issues Facing Us

The central issues facing humanity may be summarized by asking
how we can bring macro systems under ethical control and thus
create the possibility for each man and woman to have the freedom
and wellbeing to become what he/she was created to be.  In our
view, none of the existing political alternatives are adequate
to deal effectively with the problems.

The following is an attempt to categorize the problems that are
seen to exist in connection with new life styles:

a) inequality, alienation and dehumanization in our own
societies;

b) the increasing gap between the welfare of the majority in the
Northern countries and the masses in the Southern countries,
manifested in food crises, etc.;

c) pollution, resource depletion, destruction of ecosystems.

Three conflicts may be linked with these problems:

1) conflicts between classes and groups within the "developed" countries;
2) the conflict between the interests of the majority in the developed countries and those in the Third World;
3) the conflict between material interests of the present generation and the interests of future generations.

These conflicts necessitate the choosing of a position, the taking of sides. This necessity is especially clear to us in the light of the Bible. It can be said that the ultimate aim of the new life styles movement is a society in which "the right of the poor" comes first and foremost, both in personal and in societal life. This implies a concept of life styles which embraces much more than a change in individual life style alone. New life styles should be defined as attempts (usually by groups) to participate in a process of personal and social change.

2. Dilemmas

Within industrialized societies, economic and material growth has become an end in itself, to the extent that an individual's worth is measured by his/her productivity and level of consumption. These material values are so all-pervading that we even evaluate ourselves by such standards, as if spiritual values were completely irrelevant. Many of us affluent members of these societies are conscious of the incoherence between the way we know things should be and the way we actually live, and are rejecting materialism and consumerism. At the same time, a great number of deprived and powerless people in our societies are struggling for a more human material standard of living. The unjust distribution of wealth and power in our societies is the result not only of economic and political systems which reward greed, but also of the greed within each of us in seeking material rewards.

If there is inequality within industrialized countries, how much worse is the picture when we compare those countries with the nations of the so-called developing world. Some crucial economic issues facing the Third World countries are dealt with later in this report. Here we would only say that there are no obvious answers to the very vital questions challenging all countries, industrialized or not: What kind of growth? What kind of development? At what price, and who will pay that price? We plead with our sisters and brothers in the Third World not to do as we have done and improve their material conditions at the cost of destroying their spiritual and cultural gifts which could so help renewal in all societies.

Overarching all of the problems within and among nations is the relationship between all of humanity and the ecosystem, the environmental creation which allows all of us to live. Whilst applauding technological and scientific contributions to human welfare, we must seriously challenge the myth that only the so-called "experts" are competent to make decisions in these areas. It is the right and responsibility of each person to participate in decisions which affect the very existence of humanity. Among the many urgent issues, we would only mention the advance of nuclear technology with its long-living deadly waste products and potential for proliferation of nuclear weapons; the creation of artificial toxic substances which pollute the air, the water, plant and animal life on which all people depend; and the short-sighted rape of irreplaceable natural resources for our apparent immediate benefit, leaving to future generations the problem of surviving without them. To use a U.S. phrase, "There is no such thing as a free lunch." Somebody always pays, and it is incumbent upon us to ensure that wherever possible the cost falls on the person or the generation who receives the benefit.

## 3. Signs of Hope

There is growing awareness that things are not as they should be, that "there has to be a better way." In all our societies, people are beginning to share with each other their uneasiness and to find strength together to explore alternatives. Despite the apathy, despite the almost paralyzing terror that we feel as we are forced to face our own inner contradictions, the Spirit moves among us and we find courage among each other. Aware that nobody has the answers, we dare to find allies with whom we can ask new questions. Groups of church people reach out to secular movements and they begin to act together. Organizations such as trade unions, political parties and the institutional church itself are beginning to be influenced by the questions and actions of those of their members who have become aware of the need to change.

Here and there, small groups are experimenting with alternative ways of living, creating extended, non-biological "families", opening Third World shops, building solar heaters, providing alternative education for the urban poor, and soon. We can look to such experiments and see that there are indeed viable alternatives, that people have joy in "living lightly on the earth", and this may give us the hope and courage to change our own styles of living.

As we shared our experiences in our own First World countries (Australia, Federal Republic of Germany, Netherlands, Sweden, Switzerland, United Kingdom and United States), we discovered common elements in the life style movements:

a) In order to be valid, movements for a new life style should work at the same time for personal and social change. The personal example is indispensable, and it is right that we should change our own lives if we expect others to change theirs. But only if we also address ourselves to laws and regulations, to governments, parties and organizations, will we be able to influence unjust structures.

b) Those who participate in movements for a new life style are engaged in a continuous learning process. Often people start with small, marginal changes. But their experiences and the reflections which follow may lead them to greater insights and inspire them to greater courage. Learning takes time.

Reflection, encouragement and a common purpose are important. But each individual should be able to determine the speed and the ways in which he/she learns. As support for the learning process, several movements have proposed commitment to a common discipline. This relates to personal conduct as consumers, to the use of income and to the active support of political and social actions and binds the participants together.

c) Our common experience is that movements for a new life style can only last if the people concerned form groups. It is easy for the isolated individual to feel helpless and succumb to resignation. Only a group can provide the necessary direction, critique and encouragement. Groups are also more effective in motivating others and getting things done. Groups crystallize best around a precise issue, which focuses thinking and action. Such an issue, if reflected upon properly, will lead by itself to other dimensions of a new life style. At present, such issues reflect a variety of approaches on a diversity of fronts:

Some examples of actions carried out at present on the personal level

- Recycling
- Using public transport or car pools (or walking or cycling)
- Buying less processed food
- Avoiding the purchase of plastic goods
- Intentional communities (living together or not)
- Time for fun and relaxation
- Shared responsibility for the care of children, the aged and the disabled
- Finding creative alternatives to existing patterns of consumption of food and other resources
- Promoting Third World products
- Restricting personal use of energy
- Involvement in women's liberation
- Involvement in men's liberation
  etc.

Some examples of issues and actions on the structural level

- Humanizing the workplace
- Participation in decision-making at all levels
- Support of world food initiatives
- Support for UNCTAD trade initiatives
- Involvement with migrant workers
- Support for international redistribution of production (e.g., textiles)
- Political activity in favour of anti-pollution laws, better planning of land use, etc.
- Participation in the debate on nuclear technology and genetic engineering
- Political activity against militarism and the arms trade
- Support for an effective maximum/minimum incomes policy
  etc.

d) In our concern for a new life style we meet people of many convictions. Therefore, cooperation between Christians and non-Christians is mandatory. As Christians, of course, we are strongly urged by the Gospel to alter our lives, and faith reinforces our motivation. But we should be careful not to alienate through specific Christian words and actions those who do not share our belief but who recognize the common task. At the same time, Christians must be open to learning from people of different beliefs and ideologies who share the concern for new life styles.

e) So far groups have mainly sprung up from local initiatives, though in several cases they are linked to a national movement. But the more we become aware of the complexities of establishing new life styles over against the existing systems, the more urgent becomes the need for international exchange and cooperation.

## 4. An Issue for the Rich Only?

The concept of new life styles seems to have been developed mainly in the more affluent societies. This explains why the movement originally focused on consumerism, materialistic values, etc. However, it is now increasingly being placed in the much wider and more general framework of actual engagement of the people in the search for a more just, participatory and sustainable global society.

Clearly this engagement must vary in content, according to differences in the specific economic, social and political situations. In many African countries, for instance, it may imply supporting development that leads to higher levels of consumption for most people; in many European countries, on the other hand, development that involves lower levels of material consumption for many people should be supported. This is not a contradiction but follows from differences in the starting points.

## 5. Reflections from the First World

It has often been pointed out that the new life styles issue seems to be popular mainly in middle-class circles. (This does not mean that the problems necessitating a new life style exist only for those classes, but for different groups of classes the priorities may differ.) Nevertheless, for many people, conflicts within their own society (such as racial injustice) may be more urgent than ecological or development issues (both of which are major motivations in the movement for new life styles). This raises some questions. If people engaged in the search for a new life style choose to work on problems or with strategies which are different from those chosen by the working class, to what extent are these differences legitimate? To what extent are we dealing with an escape from the traditional conflicts in society?

These differences might separate the new life styles movement from other classes in society. This danger is increasingly being perceived and there are some signs that such separation can be overcome. (For example, the Dutch new life styles movement supported a boycott of South African products originally organized by the trade unions.)

It may be that middle-class people have better opportunities for discerning such problems as international maldistribution of food, energy, materials, and so on. This class enjoys a good level of comfort, leisure, security and education compared to the workers. It may well be due to a genuine concern for those who are suffering from these conflicts, rather than out of self-interest, that in the new life styles movement the ecological and development issues receive a high priority.

## 6. Reflections of a Participant from a Socialist Country

For us, living as a group in a socialist country, the question of a new life style has become relevant through considering problems of underdevelopment and of the international conflict of different social orders.

To follow Christ for us is the call to join God on his way toward man. It is the challenge to share the life of the poor because it is among them that we should seek and rediscover God. The call to discipleship will lead us also to take sides with the struggling people. By doing this we will be next to the struggling Jesus. This fight requires us to engage ourselves as partisans with those who struggle for their liberation.

Therefore, the quest for a new life style for us is the question of living in solidarity. We recognize the political meaning of solidarity. Solidarity has its firm place where progressive changes are taking place, where systems and structures which produce exploitation, oppression and injustice are changed. Solidarity means standing firmly together in order to eliminate oppression and suffering.

Solidarity with others enables us to seek a new way of life, which we call a life in solidarity. This life in solidarity is governed by two motives. First, we turn away from our egotism and consumerism and learn instead a new asceticism and simplicity. New asceticism is not to be understood as an individualistic attitude; we want to rediscover community and to consume goods together. Second, by taking sides with those who need our support, our life is enriched. Today we encounter everywhere the phenomenon of demanding things, the attitude being "this is my right," this belongs to me," and so on. In this respect solidarity is a piece of self-liberation.

With whom should we be in solidarity? With all the oppressed and exploited people; with those who liberate themselves. With whom can we not be in solidarity? With all those who are consciously woven into capitalism. Towards what aim do we use our solidarity? Towards a society in which justice lives, in which communities can grow.

54

The new life styles question is posed as if there were a corresponding concept (though in a different context and based on different assumptions) in our socialist society.

I cannot enter into theoretical reflection, but can share with you some experiences. After my theological studies I worked for seven years as a pastor in a parish. Since 1961 I have been working in a factory, as a worker in basic production units. There I see myself confronted with a different kind of reality. This reality is characterized by a basic principle: learn the socialist way, work the socialist way, live the socialist way. The concept is a socialist way of life.

In the beginning I thought I could not identify with my fellow workers. I thought that a socialist way of life was in contradiction with my Christian way of life. But I had no choice. I was simply integrated into this socialist way of life, whether I wanted or not. This forced me to reflect on the question of whether a socialist way of life and my Christian faith exclude each other or whether they coincide on certain questions.

I experience daily in my work what a socialist way of life means and want to share with you four features of it, which illustrate what that way of life really means:

a) It is guided by the principle "From I to we". All workers in the factory are members of the socialist collective. I had to ask the question whether life with others in a group is really incompatible with my Christian faith. I remembered that the Old Testament always speaks of the people of God; in the gospels we hear of the group of disciples; the epistles are mostly addressed to a congregation. I discovered that life in a group is closer to Scripture than an individualistic life. Another discovery was that Jesus Christ freed me to live with others, even in a secular group.

b) A second feature of the socialist way of life in the factory is that we are called to participate in planning, in work and in decision-making. For me this is a clear call to responsible living. My Christian faith impels me to take responsibility for my neighbours, in fact for the whole of society. Therefore, I cannot refuse concrete demands to assume responsibility.

Thus I have been directing a socialist collective for many years. I am also an elected member of the trade union leadership of my department in the factory, and a member of the commission responsible for dealing with labour conflicts. This has made it clear to me that assuming responsibility and thus participating in decision-making is possible only by joining existing socialist institutions.

c) In our factory we are clear about the fact that our work is an important contribution towards the building of a socialist society. Our long-range goal is to transform ourselves into a communist society. Thus I had only two choices: to adjust, and somehow to survive, or to decide to become committed to the goals of this society. Of course, I know that socialist society is not identical to the Kingdom of God. But society as it is programmed by socialism comes closest to our vision of the Kingdom, because it attempts to realize more peace, more justice, more liberation than other forms of social organization that I know of. Therefore, I commit myself to the building of a socialist society.

d) A last feature is that we commit ourselves to international solidarity. All members of socialist working brigades are expected to practise solidarity by giving a certain fixed percentage of their income to support groups struggling for liberation.

There are people who do this with a bad conscience, especially Christians. To me, personally, solidarity is motivated by my faith. Regarding the question of channels for development aid, I would say this is secondary. However, my experience is that, even here, cooperation between Christians and Marxists is possible. In our factory we have worked together on this issue. We have looked for a project which could be financed by "Bread for the World" (DDR).

With respect to Chile we even signed a contract with Bread for the World, but this project could not be realized, because of the military takeover. From many conversations I have come to the conclusion that development aid can be effective only if a country has already changed its social structure and is in the process of building a new society.

Right now I have to reflect seriously on what living in solidarity means in my encounter and work together with Algerian colleagues who are being trained in our factory. What does it mean to live in solidarity? More specifically, is it just sharing?

When I translate these principles into my Christian vocabulary, they signify for me that life in a group means living responsibly; that living in solidarity means living with commitment. Thus the concept of a socialist way of life often becomes an opportunity to practise my Christian faith in our particular situation.

The concept of a socialist way of life, unlike new life styles, connotes some kind of "alternative life style", because the question is not to change existing structures but to concretize and fill with life structures which have already been changed by the socialist revolution.


7. Voices from the Third World

From a Third World perspective, it may be misleading to speak about new life styles. Though the movement is concerned with the quality of economic, social and political relationships at national and international levels, the word "style" suggests that it is primarily a matter of rearranging these relations within a given framework.

In most Third World societies the question is not how to re-
arrange, but how to arrange at all.  Thus it is more appropriate
to ask what kind of life, and hence which type of social organization, is to be sought.

Some definite criteria for the kind of life desired include food
and shelter, health and education, work, participation in
decision-making processes, control (and participation in the control) over national resources and fuller participation in international, economic and political decisions.

It is quite clear that the social process aiming at these goals
is different in different countries.  In many Third World
societies it has reached an impasse.  Political and economic
power have been centred in the industrialized countries; even
with the seizing of some of that power by the OPEC nations,
decisions made in alliance with national élites in the Third
World very often clearly militate against the wellbeing of the
vast majority of poor people in the world.  Injustice and oppression prevail, with a growing trend towards authoritarian
governments, enforced by suspension of civil liberties, violation
of human rights, military regimes and torture.  These combine to
make it more and more difficult for people to struggle effectively for a meaningful life.

More justice in international relations is imperative, though
at the same time we recognize that justice within Third World
societies is far from being realized.  We need to take supportive action regarding the negotiations for a new international
economic order going on in the UN, the trade and tariff negotiations carried out in UNCTAD and GATT, commodity agreement
negotiations, the policies of the IMF and the World Bank, international code of conduct conferences (such as the Law of the
Sea, and others), business practices and policies of transnational corporations, and so on.

The new life styles movement, which is of Western origin, will
gain credibility only if it can show that it is also concerned
about changes of power relations.  These changes must come at
many levels, but not least at the level of the international
negotiations mentioned above.


8.  Unavoidable Issues

The experience of the different life style movements is revealing
at least four issues which have to be faced urgently in any discussion of the systemic changes necessary for a more just, participatory and sustainable society.

a) As was pointed out at the Fifth Assembly of the World Council
   of Churches, people are demanding greater participation in
   decision-making processes in matters affecting their lives.
   No responsible society cna exist without such full sharing by
   the people in the life of their own country, but in many
   cases their demand is violently repressed in order to maintain
   prevailing patterns of life which are not open to the new.

So the question is how to establish structures open to change, leading to a participatory society.

b) We also recognize that participation cannot be increased without certain clear guidelines which orient society and its members: people's participation does not exclude the need for planning. Furthermore, a new life style for all demands the elaboration of a plan which all, at different stages, have helped to formulate. The problem, however, is to establish the limits which should be applied to those who control the implementation of the plan in such a way that people's creativity and freedom are not diminished.

c) A major issue on which people have to decide and elaborate plans is appropriate technology. The technology imposed on production by the ruling sectors of society is not always appropriate or appropriable. Furthermore, it often helps to consolidate unevenness and disparities within and among societies, especially when inappropriate technologies are exported to underdeveloped countries. An inappropriate technology implies irresponsible use of social and natural resources, which occurs frequently in today's world. This trend needs to be corrected through a process in which the opinions of politicians, experts, workers and other people are taken into consideration - an entirely new way of dealing with this matter. The aim is not the best technology for those in power, but the best technology _for all_.

d) The quest for a new international economic order is also closely connected with the search for new life styles in local and national situations. As was said at the Nairobi Assembly: "As an effort to restructure patterns of international trade, transfer of resources, and technology, to bring about monetary reforms, and to change patterns of decision-making in international economic affairs, all geared to ensure that the poorer countries of the world have a fairer share in these matters, the new international economic order deserves to be studied carefully. However, we must not forget that at the international level there are yet no political processes to implement any radical change in the economic order and that changes in _international_ economic orders alone do not go to the roots of the problems of poverty and underdevelopment. The question is: Can a new (i.e., a more just) international economic order really be built on the basis of the present one or should it at the same time be accompanied by changes at the national level?"[1] Another question should be added: What kinds of changes in our life style are necessary to support the struggle of all people for a more just society?

It must be underlined that the issues mentioned above, like many others examined in this report, are closely interrelated, e.g., the problem of central planning is linked with the quest

---

1) Breaking Barriers: Nairobi 1975, ed. David M. Paton, SPCK, London and Wm. B. Eerdmans, Grand Rapids, 1976

for a more participatory society; discussion about a new international economic order cannot be separated from the issue of appropriate technologies and how they should be shared among peoples who need them. But discussion of the linkages and the interaction of these issues demands greater communication among peoples. Does it not call for the breaking of existing networks of information, controlled by a few, and the creation of alternative channels of communication?

## 9. Obstacles to Change

The apparently unchallengeable power of self-seeking people and institutions within our prevailing systems is a formidable barrier to change, as is the natural inertia of such systems and of all people. Fear of the unknown inhibits individuals, institutions and nations from being the first to try something new and let others gain at their expense. The material price seems too much to pay, but perhaps we fear even more the high price of losing our inner comfort, of having to examine the values and assumptions which dictate the way we conduct our lives. Here the awareness of incoherence may truly be seen as a God-sent discomfort, nagging at us until we are forced to examine ourselves, which is the necessary precondition for repentance and thus for joining in God's will for redemption. Personal change is essential, but the long struggle can only be won if we are fortified by the support and communal wisdom of others; the blessing of God is not only for the individual but for all God's people, and without each other we are less than we were created to be. But the political, social and economic structures in which individuals and groups live inevitably determine the possibilities for their liberation and empowerment; existing structures in all our countries support patterns of injustice and must be changed.

## 10. The Churches and New Life Styles

The mission of the Church implies that it has to be in the world but not of the world. Today many of our churches are part of the establishment and therefore do not react against its materialistic tendencies. In this sense, the Church has betrayed both the Lord of the Church and those whom it was meant to serve. The task of the Church today is to preach and practise love in the world, and to proclaim judgement.

The Christian Church is an institution, but it is also a community of human beings gathered for worship and sent forth to witness in the world. Many of these same human beings in their daily lives participate in decision-making that vitally affects our future.

However we define the Church, we know that it has an image and perhaps also authority in society. It is expected to have an opinion, to promote a certain way of living and to create an atmosphere which inspires the search for the new.

The churches often have great material resources. They can also mobilize people who are prepared to raise awareness and to try new life styles. They ought also to seek out and support people who are already going against the mainstream. This might be done by giving them access to the buildings, land, money and members of the Church, and by cooperating in experimental alternatives (e.g., building a solar water heater for the church, planting a communal garden on church land, supporting those who attempt to live a communal life in their development of new liturgies, etc.).

The temptation for many churches to be too much of the world is also revealed in the extravagance of their buildings, equipment, etc. Responsible stewardship of resources should be the moral guide when financial decisions, for example regarding costly restoration of church buildings, are made. The corporations, banks and other institutions in which the churches have financial interests should be closely scrutinized to determine whether such interests are in line with Christian belief. Churches should also consider the parable of the talents when dealing with their valuable possessions. In some cases there is too much of a gap between the salaries of the highest and the lowest paid among lay and ordained church employees. The churches should implement a ceiling on income and rapid equalization of salaries and should play a leading role in implementing a similar policy in secular society.

# IV. RECOMMENDATIONS TO THE CHURCHES AND TO THE WCC

## 1. Proposals for Consideration by the Churches

a) The churches are asked to consider possibilities of encouraging attempts at new life styles and of spreading and facilitating information about and among existing groups, models and experiences.

b) The churches are requested to sponsor "community laboratories" in various locations where people can begin to experience the realities of shaping a new style of life together, without the trauma of breaking up their current life style.

c) We also ask the churches to encourage their new life styles groups to rally around the issues mentioned previously in this report, and to put pressure on national decision-makers to take into account criteria of international, social and economic justice and sustainability for all people of the earth when dealing with negotiations related to UNCTAD's discussions and the new international economic order, and in national policies regarding relations with underdeveloped countries.

d) We request that the churches give symbolic support (e.g., through gestures, music, Bible interpretation, etc.) to various forms of community life which express concern for new life styles.

e) In those provinces of the church where distrust and insufficient information or stereotyped notions exist concerning the aims, motives and methods of the new life styles movement, we ask the churches to make an effort to further a climate of open and honest discussion.

f) The churches as institutions are challenged by their members' search for a new life style. How should the roles of the parish and the pastor be changed in order to support this "search for the new"? Some people feel that much of the work in the community should be done by other church-related organizations which have the necessary resources. They also consider that the pastor should not play the role of an expert in ecclesiastical work, but should integrate himself into normal life in the community.

g) In many cases, openness in the churches to considering the new life style issue may also imply rethinking their salary structures in order to demonstrate the possibilities for more equal distribution in societies in which inequalities prevail.

## 2. Proposals for the consideration of the WCC

a) We recommend that the WCC ensure that the people of the Third World begin to participate in the ongoing action-reflection programme on new life styles, especially on such issues as the search for another kind of development, the goals of growth, different types of social organization and their underlying values, the elaboration of new criteria for social organization (e.g., "the right of the poor", a society aimed at "minimizing suffering", participation, sustainability, justice).

b) We propose that the WCC facilitate sharing between alternative communities internationally. Perhaps three communities in different countries could agree to be in regular correspondence, raising issues, analyzing their community life vis-à-vis the issues and sharing their thoughts with each other. Such material could be published by CCPD for a larger network of communities. Emphasis would be on the realities of community life as informed by theological, political, philosophical, ecological and other thinking. This material would not be designed for wide distribution but for the use of communities (or communities which are forming) in criticizing and reshaping themselves.

c) We recommend that the specific contribution which "new life styles" studies and experiences can bring to the development of contextual theology be encouraged, for instance by their publication in theological magazines.

d) We ask that the WCC, through its appropriate sub-units, continue analysis of the relationship between community living and larger systemic changes. Many who are living new forms of life together have an intuitive sense that what they are doing is politically significant but are inarticulate at this point, less purposeful than they could be and at times self-doubting. CCPD could support these groups by enabling analysis and increasing our awareness of the issues as well as our role in systemic change.

e) We propose that the sub-unit on Renewal and Congregational Life, in collaboration with CCPD and the sub-unit on Dialogue with People of Living Faiths and Ideologies, develop a description of Christian community, providing criteria according to which different groups may evaluate their living together.

f) We recommend that the WCC sponsor additional international meetings with:

- smaller groups working on more specific sub-topics,
- more practitioners of alternative community living, and
- "Third World" persons.

g) We also recommend that the WCC support small-scale alternative energy projects which can be used by new communities.

3. Proposals for the consideration of CCPD

We propose that CCPD create a "Core Group on New Life Styles" (of 5 to 7 members belonging to movements involved in this kind of action) which, under the jurisdiction of CCPD, would coordinate actions and programmes between new life styles movements, groups and the WCC. As was said at the first workshop on "Alternative Life Styles" in 1975, this action-reflection process should be linked as closely as possible with the experiences and ideas that are being tested in daily practice. We request that the WCC implement this recommendation fully, to which end the proposed Core Group should work. Its main goals for action would be:

a) To provide opportunities and mechanisms for the regular sharing of experience among those actively engaged in the promotion of new life styles.

b) To enable critiques of such experiences and initiatives, especially from the perspective of the Third World.

c) To attempt to identify (in collaboration with new life styles practitioners) the major issues in the search for a "Just, Participatory and Sustainable Society", and to assist in the practical coordination of national and other initiatives and movements working on these issues.

d) To collect reports of activities and programmes which deal with these major issues, and to ensure their inclusion in the WCC's programme thrust "Towards a Just, Participatory and Sustainable Society".

e) To publish, distribute and provide for revision as necessary, an annotated list of major new life styles movements, including contact names and addresses, instructions on how to become associated with each movement, and a brief statement of its aims and scope.

f) To publicize widely the WCC's concern with the issue of new life styles.

g) To continue to publish "Dossiers" on new life styles, taking first the preparatory papers of the Glay workshop, and later:
   - descriptions of ongoing experiments
   - news of groups engaged in efforts for new life styles
   - liturgies to sensitize church groups
   - annotated bibliographies on relevant books and articles published in various languages.

h) To establish coordination between groups and people involved in the new life styles movement and programmes of the WCC which in one way or another could make a contribution to this common search (e.g., "the community of men and women," "the life of the local congregation," "urban rural mission," "just, participatory and sustainable society," "women's concerns," "spirituality and renewal," "dialogue with people of living faiths and ideologies," etc.).

## A THEOLOGICAL REFLECTION

Tissa Balasuriya

These are a few reflections in meditative form, commenting on your reports of experiences. Given the shortness of time and the vast scope of our discussions, my remarks will necessarily be limited to generalizations, for which I beg your pardon. I offer these comments with great respect for your goodwill and endeavours. They are an effort to share from another life experience. We are not responsible for our birth or the culture and history which we inherit. We can only relate to the past as given data and draw relevant conclusions for our present and future. It is clear that in this group we have a large area of agreement concerning the analysis of society and the need to concern ourselves with justice. Let us try to build on this togetherness.

### The Search for Identity

During the past few days I have been asking myself what our different searches, grouped together under the umbrella of "new life styles" are revealing. One common theme is the quest for identity. Who am I? Who are we? How can I relate to others? What is our society all about? Some of you say we cannot accept this society. Others say, "We just cannot go to this church: its worship is so unrelated to life and to the serious problems of the poor." Yet we are with the Church, and even here we visit the church. We want to fight the system, and yet we are part of it. From the United States we heard of the agony of the people of Love Canal who lead a precarious existence on a dumping site for chemical waste. From Africa we heard of a woman asking herself, "How do I relate to my family, my society, my people?" We are each questioning our own personality and experience and the society in which we live.

### The Confluence of Revolutionary Trends

One way of trying to understand this soul-searching among people is to look at the extraordinary phenomenon of several revolutionary trends which are converging and influencing each other. Alvin Toffler speaks of the process of "rapidation" in his book "Future Shock"[1].

Science and technology have advanced at a rapid pace, especially in the last few decades. The age of electronics has arrived,

---

1) Alvin Toffler, Future Shock, Bantam, New York, 1971.

bringing with it a new mode of production, which is partly the cause of the intractable problem of unemployment, even in the rich countries.

Not only has the communications revolution made us one world: it has also made us aware of the fact. There has been an explosion of information, though not necessarily of wisdom. There is thus a oneness, not only of the production process but also of knowledge, or rather information, and consequently also of our sensitivities. Travel too links us and overcomes age-old barriers between people.

These and other phenomena continue to lead us to ask fundamental questions about our own self and values. A sort of personal revolution is going on within us all: Who am I? Where am I going? Do I accept all I have been told? Do I really believe the behaviour patterns and roles imposed on us by society, tradition and religions are worthwhile? Am I concerned with the things that really count? Why are the lives of so many people and families in a mess? Why are so many societies incapable of living harmoniously?

The movement for women's liberation is world-wide in that women all over are affirming their rights as human beings. It takes different forms in different societies, but the phenomenon is becoming quasi universal. It is extremely significant in that it affects half of all humanity.

There is also a sexual revolution. We are now better able to control the process of reproduction. This gives a degree of freedom and security in relationships between persons and at the same time involves a refusal to accept some of the norms of traditional society and religions.

An equally important universal dynamic is the emergence or eruption of the poor, the subject peoples, the oppressed minorities and the despised cultures. Dominated people are acquiring a new consciousness of their dignity and their desire to be themselves as a people, culture, language group or religion. This too can be seen in every continent, irrespective of the level or type of economic development, e.g., the Basques in Spain, the Welsh in Britain, the Flemish and Walloons in Belgium, the Blacks and Indians in the Americas, the Harijans in India, the Kurds in the Middle East, the Tamils in Sri Lanka. At the same time as the world is being unified by communications and commerce, or perhaps because of it, the smaller groups are trying to affirm their identity in the modern world. There is a ferment of revolutionary movements and alliances.

Youth are another group in ferment. The young no longer assent to being considered as minors till the age of 21 and spectators in the social processes until the age of 25 or so. By 16 or 17 years of age, or even earlier, they feel they know themselves and the world and have a right to be themselves, discover their identity and even decide their own norms of behaviour and relationships.

Throughout the world there is a process of mental or cultural
liberation in which people are seeking to free themselves from
hitherto accepted superstitions, myths, practices, dogmas, faith
or values. A new consciousness that the past was not necessarily
correct in its views is leading to a spirit of questioning. Even
within Marxism there is a view that one must be anti-dogmatic in
order to be more radical and revolutionary. This again is part
of a search for authenticity, credibility and meaning. On the
one hand, it involves a desacralization of life, a breaking down
of traditional myths, and, on the other, a quest for anchorage.
What can we hold on to? What remain as permanent values? Are
we accountable to anyone for our actions? How can we cope with
the onslaught of the mass media on our lives?

This is not merely the problem of those here in this conference.
Everywhere similar questions arise. A meeting of managers,
bankers, soldiers or policemen is likely to raise similar questions. What are we about? Why should we make money, fight,
ensure security... for whose benefit? Parents and grandparents
too have problems of identity and acceptance. How do we relate
to children and grandchildren? Are we really wanted in this
society?

Religions also face revolutionary questioning. These different
forces react one with another, bringing about the very rapid
changes of our times. This makes the question of identity even
more acute. It raises questions about ultimate loyalties: to
religion, to country, to the human race, to the planet earth,
the universe, to God.

This then is the framework within which the problem of life
styles poses itself. A first step in approaching these issues
is acceptance of ourselves and of others. Both can be difficult, but are necessary. Our psychological crises are often due
to non-acceptance of ourselves. There are large areas of our
life that we cannot change, and for which we are not even responsible: our birth, sex, nationality, our natural bodily and
mental endowments, even our temperament. It is important to
realize and recognize our limits. As we grow in age these become
clearer to us.

Even more important is acceptance of the other as the other,
whether it be the other sex, the family, other age groups, races,
religions, cultures, ideologies, nature or environment. We must
respect the other in his, her or its otherness, and not expect
them to be like us, or treat them as if they existed merely for
us. The minimum requirement of this relationship is that we
should not put on others burdens which we are not prepared to
bear ourselves. Jesus condemned that attitude among the Pharisees
of his day. However, we can go much further than this in our
search for just and humane relationships with the other.

## The Life Style of Jesus

In all his relationships, Jesus brought to bear an approach of
honesty, authenticity, understanding and acceptance of the other,
rebuking evil and challenging all to spiritual growth through
selflessness. It was in the pursuit of these values that Jesus

got into trouble with the powerful of his day. He contested their values, their practices and their way of burdening the poor people for their own advantage. The Sabbath, he said, is made for man, and not man for the Sabbath. They disapproved of his life style of openness and friendship towards all, including the social outcasts.

His way of teaching also involved a new life style. He taught credibly because he practised what he taught. He presented his teaching consistently, fearlessly, unwaveringly, tirelessly and within the situations of life of his people. Opposition did not frighten him or make him give up or run away. He did not present facile quick solutions or political messianism of a kingdom of Israel to be restored in the immediate future: what he gave was basic institution into the nature of human life and the fact that our fulfilment comes through accepting others as ourselves. All power and authority is for service to others. The Son of Man did not come to be served but to serve (cf. Mark 10:42-45).

Jesus invited his disciples to follow him on this road to spiritual growth through unselfish self-giving to others. He commissioned them to carry this message to the corners of the earth: "The disciple is not greater than the master; I have washed your feet, you should do likewise." This act has a deep symbolism, being one of his final actions with the disciples. It manifests a life style of servanthood and service. Jesus also warned the disciples that in following him they would be persecuted: "They have hated me, they will hate you." "If you do not take your cross and follow me, you are not worthy of me." This is a sort of criterion of discipleship. If, in situations of injustice, the disciples of Jesus were not opposed by those who benefited from injustice, it would be an indication that they were not communicating his message properly, and if the disciples were, either directly or indirectly, to support and legitimise the oppressors, they would be compromising the Gospel of Jesus.

## Jesus Challenges the Rich

It is often debated whether the Good News of Jesus is for all, both rich and poor, oppressor and oppressed. If the Gospel brings good news to all, it does so in diverse ways, making different challenges to different people. The gospel texts make it clear that Jesus put very strong challenges to the rich. He was particularly critical of their life styles insofar as the possession of things implied sinfulness, an inordinate attachment to them. You cannot serve God and Mannon. The idolatry (i-dollar-try) of money and the craze for power were two evils which he condemned as dehumanizing persons and hence dishonouring God.

We are familiar with the story of the rich young man who came to Jesus seeking the path to greater perfection. He asked, "What should I do? What should my life style be?" Jesus replied, "Keep the commandments." The young man said, "I have done all these things; what more need I do?" Jesus then proposed a more difficult life style: "Sell all that you have .... and come and follow me." The young man was not prepared to do this, as he was extremely rich. Is this the sort of challenge that is addressed to

us also - especially in the affluent countries? The call of
Jesus is to be converted like Zacchaeus, who gave half his wealth
to the poor and repaid fourfold whatever he had taken unjustly.
Jesus, then, had contact with the rich, but in a way that did not
compromise his message but rather called them to a genuine change
in life style. He was categorical in his denunciation of the
lawyers, Pharisees and rulers. His language was so strong that
one wonders whether someone writing such things today would not
be regarded as unholy or unchristian, and be accused of being
unbalanced, insolent, communist.

## Jesus Preached the Kingdom of God

Jesus gave as the touchstone for admission to the Kingdom of
Heaven a life style of unselfish service. "I was hungry and you
gave me to eat... You may enter the Kingdom because you served
others, and thus loved me; for I identify with the suffering
poor." The prerequisite of following Jesus is not merely saying
"Lord, Lord..." or being a nominal Christian, but loving service
to others. Jesus explained his mission as the liberation of
those in difficulty, of the oppressed. "The spirit of the Lord
is upon me because he has anointed me; he has sent me to announce
good news to the poor, to proclaim release for prisoners and
recovery of sight for the blind; to let the broken victims go
free, to proclaim the year of the Lord's favour." (Luke 4:18-19)

A correct understanding of the mission of the followers of Jesus
in these terms is important. It is a call to new values, a new
life, a new life style, and hence to a change in society also.
This liberation is of the very substance of the Christian mission
and implies an ecclesiology which is different from the theology
of the Church that has prevailed for many centuries.

## The Life Style of the Apostles

Jesus founded a group of disciples to continue and expand his
work. From their way of life we get an indication of how those
closest to Jesus understood both him and his message. They were
united in the sharing of goods, the breaking of bread, in worship and witness to Jesus Christ. Joining their group involved
a rupture with the values prevailing in the society of that time,
especially the Roman Empire. They had to renounce idolatry of
wealth, subservience to power and discrimination against human
beings on the basis of social status, nationality, etc. They set
up communities of believers as real human fellowships. So contrary to the traditional society were these that Christians were
more or less underground groups. They were in effect contesting
the consumerist, pleasure-seeking values of the Roman Empire
that provided "bread and circuses" (panem et circenses) for
their citizens - at the price of their numerous slaves.

The early Christian life style was so contrary to that of the
affluent Romans that the latter found the disciples of Jesus a
nuisance, an influence which they could not domesticate. The
Christian way of life was thus a contesting of the socio-political
and economic principles and policies of the ruling patricians of
the day. The Christian faith was therefore considered a danger

to the Empire and Christians were persecuted. Martyrdom was not infrequent in Christian groups. Their convictions about Jesus, his way of life and promise of eternal life were so strong that they were not afraid to suffer for their faith or, indeed, to give it the supreme testimony of their lives. Even the early structuralization of the Church did not go against this life of giving oneself for others: bishops and popes headed the lists of martyrs, and rising in ecclesiastical rank meant being more susceptible to suffering at the hands of the ruling powers.

## Conversion to Empire

The life style of Christians, especially of church leaders, changed greatly as they became more identified with the ruling powers, after the mutual conversion of Christianity and the Roman Empire. The religious inspiration diminished as the institution became more and more swayed by the values of the Empire. Even subsequent monasticism was unable to prevent the weakening - if not corruption - of Christian motivation. During later feudal times, Christianity adapted itself to the social system, with some influence for the better, but held captive by its limitations.

A much worse relationship developed as European power expanded to other continents, from the sixteenth century onwards. The growth of scientific knowledge, technological power and wealth led to the European invasion of the other continents. For the peoples outside Europe these were a sort of "Barbarian Invasion" in which so much of what they valued was destroyed by European pirates, soldiers, merchants and settlers in their lands. In this process human values were completely subordinated to the rapacity of the expanding European peoples. Unprecedented brutality swept the face of the earth and can still be seen today in the remnants of colonial empires, e.g., in South Africa.

The sad reality is that Christian values and life styles were adapted to accompany, legitimize and benefit from this heinous European imperial enterprise. European economic growth was intimately linked with the cruel exploitation and even extermination of other peoples. Christian theology adjusted itself to live comfortably with this robbery and genocide. A theory of mission was evolved in which salvation was made dependent upon the presence and ministrations of Christian clergy, which in effect meant the European clergy, and colonial expansion and empire-building received a providential sanction from its relationship to the missionary enterprise.

Thus we see the extent of the vitiation of both Christian life and thought by the love of gain at the expense of others. This was totally contrary to the teachings and life of Jesus and the early Christians. The Protestant Reformation, which divided Christianity, did not reduce the dependence of the life style of Christians on local and foreign exploitation. Protestantism did challenge certain abuses of power within the Church, but it did not oppose the political economy of imperialism and capitalism. In some respects the so-called "Protestant ethics" made a ritual of material prosperity, without much concern about the means used to attain it. The foreign mission activities of the churches were well motivated, but not directed to contesting the false

values of European invasions; thus schools and health and social
services were marginal to the mainly exploitative relationships
of peoples.

This unbridled development of local capitalism and foreign imperialism went on for over four centuries, from about 1500 to
1945, and had a profound influence on European and North American
Christian life. The churches were subordinated to the process
of European enrichment and thus neglected justice. Christian
sanctification was considered a personal matter, unrelated to
what happened in society around. Spirituality was made strangely
other-worldly. The sacraments were interpreted without relevance
to social life and witness. Ecclesiastical power was on the
side of the powerful national establishments. The virtues ex-
tolled were of a passive nature: obedience, submission, docility,
regularity, patience. Jesus himself was presented as meek and
mild, gentle and patient, obedient unto death. It was the
"sweet heart of Jesus" spirituality. Mary his mother was seen
as the humble handmaid of the Lord, saying "yes" to every situation. Christian morality concentrated on sexual ethics while
turning a blind eye to the ongoing robbery and genocide.

The life styles within the Church were developed so as to fit
into this overall situation, without challenging its inhumanity.
Thus religious congregations and orders born in this period were
all implicitly subservient to capitalistic relations of life,
even though extraordinarily well motivated. Their views of
sanctity were void of social analysis and they were hence able
to coexist with brutal exploitation of the European working
classes, the colonized peoples and the slaves in the Americas.

In the history of the churches, the rise of monasteries and
various orders and religious congregations was an effort to work
out relevant life styles in their day. In present times we have
seen a rapid decline in the number of priests and religious
living in communities. Is this a sign that, at least in the form
in which they were constituted, they are losing their relevance
and appeal? They no longer represent the radical edge of the
Christian experience. They do not even demand hard options of
life style. This may be why young people of goodwill are not so
attracted to traditional religious groups, unless they are seen
as a means of getting away from it all - as a _fuga mundi_.

The new life styles movement is an indication that the Spirit is
expressing itself in new ways. It can be seen in all parts of the
world. Celibacy was traditionally a fundamental condition for
Christian dedication through a life of consecration. Today
attitudes towards family life and interelations among the sexes
have changed so much that it is difficult to see how the traditional form of celibacy could be a meaningful basis of a large-
scale movement for renewal of life styles. It is a joyful bur-
geoning of the Spirit in our times that so many married couples
and families want to devote themselves to others in a search for
new ways of Christian life and witness. The conditions of modern
life make for a much greater intermingling of the sexes in both
work and dwelling place. Corresponding to this situation, many
different groups of people are found in new life styles groups.
"Communes" are another life style, especially popular among the

accumulated in the hands of a few overlords of the international-
ized production and trade system.

Both the individual person and social groups then are deeply
afflicted. Human unrest is caused not only be our unavoidable
infirmities and mortality, but also by the folly of our self-
destructive injustice. Now we are aware of these things and this
compounds our problems. If we did not know that our life style
destroyed others, we would not need to feel so guilty. But
today the media, through their very extravagance, bring these
realities right into our living room. Refugees and victims of
famine appear at our breakfast table. The UN World Food Council,
due to meet in Ottawa in the summer of 1980, has confirmed that
50 million people starve to death each year. The world food
shortage is described as "genocide without precedent in human
history".

In our two-thirds-world countries we see this regularly - if we
have the eyes to see. People rot in the slums and shanty towns
which contain a third of Asia's free-world poor urban inhabitants.
Tea and coffee are cheap drinks all over the world because the
plantation workers live or are kept as beasts of burden on the
estates. Life is brutal and short for the poor in our poor
countries. The unnecessary deaths of so many children in the
Colombo shanties haunt me, as I think of these issues. The indifference of those who are in a position to do something is even
more shocking. We feel powerless in the face of the enormity of
these crimes. How many women in our countries are unable to
develop to the fullness of their humanity because of discrimination against young girls and females - from birth to death!
These are our sisters, our mothers. What ignorance, helpless-
ness, malnutrition and starvation pervade our lands! The cost
of one day's issue of the New York Times would provide school
books for all the children of Nicaragua for a whole year.

The Gospel from the Poor

As Christians we can ask ourselves what the Scriptures and the
situation of the world's poor have to tell those of us who seek
relevant life styles and credible forms of Christian witness.
The Gospel is a message of liberation to all, especially the
poor, the weak and the oppressed, and it is the poor who can best
reveal to us the radical demands of the Gospel today. In that
sense the poor can open the Gospels for us. They can evangelize
us. Jesus is more identified with, and suffering in them. They
can also tell us how much our life styles need to change to be
truly evangelical. Those who are in danger of being unspiritual
are the oppressors, who are generally also the affluent. The
rich need to hear the saving message from the condition of the
poor.

This means that persons from rich countries and in affluent situations cannot credibly present Christ or represent him among
the poor unless they contest the evils in their own position
and in society. Thus the mission of the Church itself is tied
to the question of new life styles, and to struggles to change
social structures, especially in the rich countries. In the

Asian, African and Latin American countries too we have to question the life style of the élites, which is often the cause of the misery of the masses. The earlier activities of churches, e.g., schools and social services, did not often help reduce inequalities and injustices. In that sense they may have been counter-witnesses to the values of the Kingdom as presented by Jesus. The churches have therefore to place the question of life styles, especially those of their full-time workers and ministers, in the forefront of the process of their renewal.

In the churches, as in society, the life styles of members and their mission of societal action need to be integrated. It is not enough to be poor: we need to join in the struggle of the poor for their liberation. This raises questions of alliances of Christians with others engaged in the same cause. The examples of Christian groups active for liberation in Nicaragua and Zimbabwe point to practical ways of interrelation - even though each historical situation has its ambiguities and should never be equated with the Kingdom of God on earth.

## The Hope of the Poor

Listening to the reports and discussions here one gets an impression of the hopelessness of the world situation. The rich are not only unwilling to change their life styles that others may live, they are even prepared to fight to defend their privileges. It looks as if injustices will continue and even worsen in the coming decades.

Yes, from the point of view of the history of the masses in the past half century, the poor and weak peoples of the world have awakened to become the architects of their own destiny. The peoples, cultures, religions and especially women, who have been submerged, despised and marginalized for millenia, are rising to a consciousness of their dignity and rights. At times this bursts forth into revolutionary thrusts - with all their hopes and dilemmas. There is also the normal, gradual awakening that is bearing fruit in different parts of the world, imperceptibly but really. The resurgence of Islam during the 1970s is one powerful instance of such motivation and mobilization of people. No amount of armaments - not even nuclear weapons - can prevent, for instance, the Black people of South Africa from ridding themselves of White domination. These struggles, despite their ambiguities, are the hope of the poor. Christians have very often been on the side of the oppressors. It is our hope that the new life style movements will take their stand on the side of the oppressed and push or pull the churches along with them.

## A New World Order

For the poor peoples of the world hope lies in the effective change of the present system of nation states into a true world community in which human beings themselves count, and not mere money or power. The present international order is the result of violence - the piracy and imperial expansion of Europe in the past few centuries. One of the most blatant injustices in the world is the maldistribution of land to population. The present

world (dis)order in which nearly a billion people live in China
and another 650 million in India, with only 14 million in
Australia and 22 million in Canada, is a situation which calls
to heaven for radical transformation.  The racism of this situation is on a far larger scale than that of apartheid in South
Africa, though it is not as consciously realized in world public
opinion..  It cannot continue for ever: the very force of population will break these frontiers of racism.

The population planning policies so powerfully thrust on us by
the rich countries are another consequence of the selfishness of
the affluent.  Rather than share their lands and provide more
work and wealth for everybody, they want the population of the
poor countries - i.e., non-whites - to decrease.  They speak of
the world being short of resources and yet spend $500 billion
annually on armaments.  This is enough to make life worth living
for 500 million people, or to develop vast new areas of the
earth's surface for tens of millions of people.  The blindness
of so many in this regard is a measure of the failure of the
people of goodwill to influence world opinion.  Of course there
should be rational population planning, and this will influence
life styles, but it must be within the wider world planning of
resource utilization and sharing.

Though the capitalistic system and values are the major cause of
the present ills of the world, the culture of the Western
European peoples has many valuable features, such as the spirit
of scientific inquiry, freedom, democracy and human rights.
These form part of the patrimony of humanity.  The socialist
countries, which accentuate equality and justice, also have much
to learn from the liberal democratic traditions of Western
Europe and North America.  These two types of life style have
much to contribute to each other.  The traditional way of life of
the peoples of the Orient and Africa and the suppressed peoples
of the Americas and Oceania have other complementary values,
such as concern for the human person, the community and nature,
which could also beneficially influence human life styles everywhere, if they are not destroyed before their worth is realized.

## A Global Role for Christians

Within this massive search and thrust of humanity, the Christian
churches could play a most creative role.  For this we have to
be freed by the liberating spirit of the gospel from our captivity to selfish barbarism.  We need to meet in small groups of
the neighbourhood or of similar interests and be motivated by
the gospel and the reality around us.  These small groups must
be linked to wider alliances, nationally and internationally.
Since Christians are present almost everywhere in many continents
of the world we could thus be a powerful ally in this process of
world-wide human liberation.  Our presence both at the grass
roots and in the centres of power and decision-making could give
added strength to these movements.  The true ecumenism of the
future will thus be across denominations, religions and ideologies, in the unselfish and critical service of the emerging new
humanity.  The new life style groups could be one stream contributing to this universal search.

74

younger generation. These are often formed for a common cause, with or without a religious motivation. The churches need to listen to what the Spirit is telling us through this groping search for alternative ways of living without being coopted by the overpowering social system and traditional ecclesiastical structures. The churches could be of sorely needed support to them.

## Nemesis of a Civilization

What we have been witnessing in recent decades is disillusionment with a civilization which is based on exploitation of the many by the few, and of nature, with little regard for its conservation. There is a profound crisis in economic and political life due to the inability of even the rich countries to resolve their problems of inflation, rising cost of living and continuing mass unemployment, the uncontrollable nature of the transnational economic giants, monopolization of the media, large-scale pollution of the environment, the squandering on armaments and the threat of nuclear extermination. The sense of isolation and meaninglessness of life in highly urbanized, consumeristic societies is felt even more intimately. Selfishness has become so intensified, life so materialistic and values so calculating that people have very little time for others. The handicapped and the aged often feel unwanted - a burden on society. Women particularly are degraded and made instruments of pleasure and commerce. Nature itself is protesting against a type of development which is leading to rapid exhaustion of non-renewable resources and proliferation of chemical and biological waste that is harmful to all life.

The fundamental error in all this is that civilization is pushing human selfishness to an extreme, without concern for nature, other peoples or even the persons nearest us. We have no regard for the other, we are unconcerned about what happens to others: all that count are our own comforts. This is the basic error of the capitalistic way of life. Feudalism and the life styles of the native peoples of Asia, Africa, the Americas and Oceania were communitarian. The land belonged to all. People cared for each other as a group, though they too had their forms of exploitation. Socialism also is based on collective concern for the essential needs of all. As such it is a protest against the evils of capitalistic exploitation. Yet in socialistic societies too there remain unresolved problems of accountability of power.

The exploitation of the rest of the world by the affluent one third is also leading to a breakdown in international economic relations. Europe, North America and Japan cannot go on increasing their standard of living for ever, for the poor cannot afford to subsidize them indefinitely. They are protesting in diverse ways: social revolutions, OPEC-type producer cartels, economic competition from new industrialized countries all challenge the hegemony of the so-called First and Second Worlds. The poorer life style of the Asians enables them to compete with the high cost products of the affluent countries, but transnationally, capitalism benefits in a new way, from both low wage producers and high price consumers. In this process both are exploited and an enormous amount of unaccountable capital is

75

The example of Nicaragua is significant in this respect. The Christian groups saw the problems of the people, but did not have the methodology of action. The Sandinistas provided the mode of revolutionary struggle against the 45-year-old dictatorial rule of the Somoza family. Gradually Christian groups joined the Sandinistas and eventually the dictator and his foreign allies were overthrown. A joint effort is now being made to build a new Nicaragua, with Christians cooperating in motivation and implementation. Like every human effort, it will have its difficulties and ambiguities. But it is in the midst of such trying realities that we have to take our stand. The decisions of the Christians of Nicaragua and Zimbabwe were niether easy nor pleasant. They got quasi universal acclaim only after victory - not during the struggle, when the world's media dubbed them "rebels" and "terrorists".

What a powerful motivation Christianity could be for justice and sharing among people, if the Sunday Eucharist were genuinely Christ-like! About 100 million people meet weekly in our churches and communities all over the globe. This is the world's largest and most regular mass meeting. It is up to us to use it to build God's Kingdom on earth.

In all this, suffering will inevitably be the lot of the disciples of Jesus. Our search for new life styles then must include preparedness for the ultimate sacrifice of life itself. This is the lesson of Jesus. Mahatma Gandhi had long been accustomed to imprisonment, prior to his martyrdom. Martin Luther King and Archbishop Romero are two other modern martyrs, symbolizing countless others. Kim Chi Ha, the poet, of Korea says that when we are ready to die, then we can also face the other trials of life with equanimity. If we follow the crucified Master in the service of others, then the sacrifice of material advantages will be nothing compared with the joy and peace of such service.

Even more important than preparedness to die is determination to struggle for truth and justice. To persevere in struggle, in spite of weaknesses and failures, is more difficult than to die. Death is once and for all, living for others is a continuous dying of self; a self giving. To opt for the side of the poor, as Jesus did, is a sort of death to the privileges of affluence; it is foolishness according to the wisdom of the world. It is the folly of the cross today.

But it is precisely the weak ones of the world that the Lord strengthens. The alliance of the just can reduce the empires of the unjust. Martyrdom can be reduced by linkages. Amnesty International, through its world-wide network and untiring universal diligence, has set many thousands of captives free. It has also brought judgement on the unjust rulers of our times.

The churches, with these life style groups, can place their collective strength on the side of the poor in their struggle for personhood, dignity, identity and life itself. What a glorious mission this is for the World Council of Churches and all disciples of Jesus. Our universality would then be a blessing to humanity and a witness to the liberating love of God revealed in

Jesus.  We would be valuable spaces of freedom; our life style
groups would give a foretaste of the joys of the Kingdom to be
realized.  We can participate in the effort to build a quali-
tatively new phase of human history that transcends the narrow
limits of ourselves, our churches and national frontiers and
thus respond to God who speaks to us in truth and spirit.  Our
search for new life styles is part of this process.  Our lives
will have meaning when we try to live for others.  My fulfilment
is in my effort to see that I do not take so much that others
cannot live; that I do not so behave that others are not ful-
filled.  And, in this, Jesus of Nazareth gives us a motivation,
for he says, "I came that you may have life and life abundantly"
and "This is my commandment: Love one another.  Greater love
than this hath no man, that he give his life for his friends."
"Do this in remembrance of me."

ELEMENTS FOR A BIBLIOGRAPHY ON NEW LIFE STYLES

prepared for the concluding consultation on
New Life Styles, Gallneukirchen, Austria,
May 5-12, 1980, by IDOC International Rome,
on behalf of CCPD.

revised and updated, October 1980.

"Our final concern in the 1980s should be to keep human

life human under the stresses and opportunities of

economic growth.  Such a strategy for development

should yield positive results in the lives of people,

whom, in moving poetry, Rabindranath Tagore has

identified as the poorest, the lowliest, the exploited,

and the lost."

from Into the 1980s: Some Ecumenical Views on the
Challenges to Values and Structures, report of the
meeting of the CCPD/WCC Advisory Group on Economic
Matters, Le Cénacle, Geneva, January 9-14, 1980,
chapter IV: "Structural Changes in Developing
Countries".

The following bibliography is an attempt to replace the new
life styles issues within the wider context of the ecumenical
debate on development. The key concepts behind such a debate
are justice, participation and sustainability, while the biblical perspective leads to an always clearer option for the poor
and the oppressed. The bibliography follows the headlines of
the basic document for the Gallneukirchen Consultation: A concluding Consultation on New Life Styles (Document No. 7a, WCC/
CCPD Officers' Meeting, Geneva, 7-9 December 1979). It presents
only some of the issues to be addressed. Other issues could be
mentioned: hunger and the land problem, new communities, health
and toxics, etc.

This bibliography can also be considered as a companion to
Towards a Church in Solidarity with the Poor, a document of the
World Council of Churches, with an annotated bibliography by IDOC
International, 96 pp., April 1980.

Documents listed in the previous CCPD dossiers on New Life
Styles are not mentioned here.

\* \* \* \* \* \* \*

I.   Into the Eighties and Beyond: Trends in macro economics

     1. Reports
     2. Future Studies
     3. The New Technology and the Future

II.  The Development Debate

     1. Basic Needs, People's Participation and the NIEO
     2. Some Initiative Towards Alternative Patterns of
        Development and Life Styles
     3. IFDA: The Search for Development Alternatives
     4. Ecodevelopment

III. Some Problem Areas: Movements and Counter-Movements

     1. The Threat of Death: Militarism and the Armaments Race
     2. The Nuclear Debate
     3. Multinational Corporations
     4. Environment Movements
     5. The Women's Movement
     6. Ethnic Minorities and Indigenous Peoples
     7. Consumer Action

IV.  Towards a New Ethics - NLS and the Churches

     The Emergence of a New Ethics
     The Role of the Churches

# I.  INTO THE EIGHTIES AND BEYOND: TRENDS IN MACRO ECONOMICS

## 1.  Reports

Interfutures, Final Report - Facing the Future: mastering the probable and managing the unpredictable, Organization for Economic Cooperation and Development (OECD), Paris, June 1979, 450 pp. This report examines future prospects for industrialized societies, taking into account possible developments in the Third World.  In the industrialized world, the report notes the aspirations to new life styles, namely in the fields of the use of time, of participation in decision making, of labour and leisure, of family, culture, and ecology.  At this point, however, it is still impossible to say in how much this will produce a deeper transformation at the level of values and consequently whether a new model of society will emerge.  Four great technological enterprises are currently under way: telematics, biology, oil substituting energy, utilization of the oceans and of space.  Deep structural changes are foreseen.  The authors of the report describe four future scenarios: strong growth, mdoerate growth, North-South rupture, protectionism.  The most probable one is, according to them, moderate growth.  But it is divided in two hypotheses: the first is the emergence of new values; the second is the continuation of the present model.

International Development Strategy, The Stanley Foundation, Porvoo, Finland, 24-25 June 1979, English, 50 pp. The 14th Conference on the United Nations in the Next Decade, sponsored by the Stanley Foundation, discussed the topic of an "International Development Strategy", in the light of the first two development decades (the 60s and the 70s) and in view of the 1980 Special Session of the UN General Assembly on international development.  The concept of mutuality of interest was basic to the conference: "some have tended to regard economic development as a process in which the gains of one group of nations might be the losses of another...  A continuation of the present trends will result in a world which is hopelessly popularized by the year 2000."

World Development Report, The World Bank, Belgrade, October 1979

In his address to the Board of Governors, World Bank President Robert McNamara draws the lessons of the second development decade, stating that "the international development community really has no adequate means to implement agreed-upon development policy."  He then considers some of the critical development problems to be faced in the 1980s and beyond.  The report assesses the problems and prospects that arise in four principal areas: the employment challenge, the importance of achieving balance and complementarity between agriculture and industry, the massive new tasks posed by the unprecedented rate of urban growth and the need to restore a more supportive international environment for trade, capital flows and energy development.

William C. Thiesenbusen, The Eighties: Will They Be the Decade of the Peasant? in "Land Reform, Land Settlement and Cooperatives", No. 1, FAO, Rome, 1979.

Signs point to change which might occur in the 1980s in rural areas:

1. peasants are becoming better organized;
2. the "demonstration effect" of token development programmes will soon be exhausted;
3. the "technology of repression" may be reaching its limits;
4. so also the overcrowding of the cities following the rural-to-urban migration due to a lack of positive programmes to deal with peasants;
5. religious leaders can no longer be relied upon to be unequivocal conservatives;
6. even businesses and middlepersons realize that the internal market must be expanded if they are to prosper;
7. the emergence of China in the world scene will publicize the model it followed to feed itself apparently without mass starvation, in conditions of substantial autarchy, apparently minimal brutality, and utilizing mainly locally developed technology.


Outlook for World of Labour in 1980s, International Labour Office, 5 February 1980.

The ILO Medium-Term Plan for the 1982-1987 period foresees labour problems becoming more complex and acute. The world workforce will total 2,045 million by the end of 1987 (an increase of 250 million, nine-tenths of which will occur outside agriculture, the cities of the Third World growing by 390 million inhabitants by 1987). Mass poverty is the most critical labour problem of the new decade. "In the industrialized North around 60 million jobs will have to be created between 1980 and the end of 1987 both to absorb those joining the workforce and to eliminate existing unemployment. But in the industrializing South nearly 600 million new jobs will be needed to give each member of the workforce an income adequate to meet his own minimum basic needs and those of his family." The danger is that many countries will be strongly tempted to minimize the importance of basic human rights in labour matters which were extensively violated in the 1970s! Few of these problems can be solved without a fundamental change in international economic relations aiming at giving the developing countries their fair share of the world's economic opportunities.


North-South: A Program for Survival, by the Independent Commission on International Development Issues (the Brandt Commission), c/o ISS, 251 Badhuisweg, NL-2509 The Hague, the Netherlands, 12 February 1980.

This commission was created in 1977. Its members are senior politicians from both developed market economy countries and developing countries. The final report was submitted to the UN Secretary-General on 12 February 1980.

The Report touches issues such as agriculture, population, environment, disarmament and development, commodities, energy, Third

World industrialization, multinational corporations and the international monetary crisis. It puts forward a "new approach to development finance", i.e., a more universal and automatic system of international burden-sharing. An emergency programme is then outlined for the period 1980-1985; increasing official aid by $8 billion a year (a rise of nearly a third); doubling the World Bank's lending; using IMF gold stocks to raise money for lending (inter alia) to the poorest countries at lowered rates of interest; an energy strategy imposing obligations on both producers and consumers; a global food programme putting money into developing country agriculture.

## 2. Future Studies

BOOKS (quoted and reviewed in "Development Forum", January-February 1980)

Christopher Freeman and Marie Tahoda, <u>World Futures: The Great Debate</u>, Martin Robinson, London, 1978, 416 pp.

International inequality and growth levels as they affect food, energy, non-renewable resources and technology are examined. The authors maintain that diffusion of the best available technological know-how could deal with many current world problems. War and the arms race remain the most important problem for the future.

Hazel Henderson, <u>Creating Alternative Futures: The End of Economics</u>, Berkeley Publishing Corporation, New York, 1978.

Tackling key economic and ethical issues of the day, Ms Henderson expounds the dangers of centralization and the advantages of "human scale" undertakings.

Fred Emery, <u>Futures We Are</u>, Martinus Nijhoff Social Sciences Division, P.O. Box 33, Leiden, the Netherlands, 1979, 230 pp.

The author argues that there are already powerful pressures to debureaucratize society and recognition of the greater efficiency of organizing work around groups within the "own territory" and without an internal status hierarchy. Characterizing the present age as one of turbulence he examines adaptive and maladaptive models likely to appear and develop to cope with it.

<u>The Conserver Society: A Workable Alternative for the Future</u>, Harper and Row, New York, 1979, 286 pp.

Sponsored by two governments and 14 government agencies, the study describes five possible scenarios - doing more with less, more with more, the same with less, less with less, and less with more. A realistic goal is a society that conserves rather than squanders, one in which we conserve without feeling deprived.

Alternatives to Growth I: A Search for Sustainable Futures,
Ballinger, Cambridge, Massachusetts, 1979, 405 pp.

First of five volumes of papers by leading environmentalists
chronicling the evolution of imaginative research on constructive
alternatives to growth. The contributors look at nutrition and
energy, economic alternatives in an age of limits, the politics
of equity and social progress in a finite world and life styles
and social norms for a sustainable state as they may, of necessity, characterize life in the last decades of this century.


OTHER BOOKS (among those used for the National Ministries En-
visioning Conference, American Baptist Convention, January 28-30,
1980)

Don Glines, compiler, Educational Futures, Vol. I: Imaging and
Inventing; Vol. II: Options and Alternatives; Vol. III: Change
and Reality; Vol. IV: Updating and Overleaping; Educational
Futures Projects, Sacramento, California, Anvil Press, Millvill,
Minnesota, 1978.

K.E. Goodpaster and K.M. Sayre, eds., Ethics and Problems of the
21st Century, University of Notre Dame Press, Notre Dame, London,
1979.


RESOURCES: SPECIALIZED INSTITUTIONS

| | |
|---|---|
| The World Future Society | 4916 St. Elmo Avenue (Bethesda) Washington, D.C. 20014, USA |
| The World Future Studies Federation | Secretariat: Casella Postale 6203 Roma-Prati, Italy |
| Association Internationale Futurible | 55 rue de Varennes, F-75007 Paris, France |
| International Creative Center publisher of "Futurology" | 20 ch. Colladon CH-1209 Geneva, Switzerland |
| The Canadian Association of Future Studies | 302-100 Gloucester St., Ottawa, Ontario K2P OA4, Canada |

The Fifth Annual Conference of CAFS was also the Third General
Assembly of the World Future Society. Its theme was Through the
80s: Thinking Globally Acting Locally.

| | |
|---|---|
| Swedish Secretariat for Futures Studies | Regeringsgatan 65, P.O; Box 7502 S-103 92 Stockholm, Sweden |
| Future Studies Centre | 15 Kelso Road, Leeds LS2 9PR, United Kingdom |
| Gamma, Montreal/McGill University Future Studies Group | C.P. 6128, Montreal 101, P.O., Canada |

## 3. The New Technology and the Future

**The Future Impact of Computers: a Twenty Year View**, ed. by Michael
L. Dertouzos and Joel Moses, MIT Press, Cambridge, Massachusetts,
September 1979.

**The Perversion of Science and Technology, An Indictment**, World
Order Models Project, 1978, English, 8 pp.
A statement by an international group of scientists on the role
of scientific and technological development in western cultural-
colonial expansion and the exploitation of the Third World.

**Lenny Siegel, Microelectronics Does Little for the Third World**,
in: "Pacific Research", Fast Palo Alto, California, Second Quarter
1979, English, 7 pp.
"Export-led industrialization" is today probably the most popular
development strategy among international financial circles and
the Asian technocrats that follow their recommendations. The
rise of this strategy has coincided with the rapidly expanding
demand - in the developed nations - for semiconductor electronics
components. Though export-led industrialization generally brings
expanded GNP, employment and foreign exchange earnings, it also
generates numerous problems. It increases dependence on foreign
capital, technology and markets; it disrupts the social fabric of
host country; and it diverts domestic resources to service foreign
economic interests. It is not, in general, an optimum strategy
for improving the economic conditions for the populations of poor
nations.

**The New Technology**, "CIS Anti-Report No. 23", Counter-Information
Services, London, 1979, English, 40 pp.
A special issue on the microelectronics revolution and its impact
on labour, with basic information on the companies operating in
this sector. Microelectronics and employment problems: the job
losses, especially in Britain and within the post offices. The
massive profits of U.S. multinationals producing computers and
telecommunication apparatus. Investments in the Third World
(especially in S.E. Asia and E. Asia): the exploitation of cheap
labour.

**Linda Y.C. Lim, Women Workers in Multinational Corporations: the
Case of the Electronics Industry in Malaysia and Singapore**,
Michigan Occasional Paper No. IX, Fall 1978, Department of Economics, Swarthmore College, University of Michigan, Ann Arbor,
60 pp.
This paper examines the multinational electronics industry in its
two most favoured off-shore locations, Malaysia and Singapore,
from the perspective of a political economy analysis of women's
employment. It analyzes the reasons for the sudden high and sustained **demand** on the part of the multinationals for female labour
in developing countries, while examining also the particular historical conditions in both host countries which led to government

encouragement of investment by the international industry, and the creation of a supply of female wage labour for the electronics (and other labour-intensive) factories.

Bruno Lamborghini, The Diffusion of Microelectronics in Industrial Companies, 1979, English and Italian, 21 pp.

"The effect of microelectronics currently most in evidence appears to be the reduction of employment in some industrial activities, but this is only the tip of the iceberg. The submerged part (effects on productivity, new applications, impact on users, creation of new professional skills, 'production' of information and 'information society') contains several indistinct elements which have considerable potential."

Employment and Technology, report by the TUC General Council to its 1979 Congress, London, September 1979, English, 71 pp.

"The impact of the new technology on employment in the 1980s is one of the greatest challenges facing us... The trade union movement too has a more demanding role to play today than 100 years ago." The report deals with the following issues: the development and the application of new technology; job prospects and the immediate impact; aspects of manpower and educational policies; trade union education; checklist of negotiators.

Microprocesseurs et robots. Les effets de la technologie moderne sur les travailleurs, comité central de la FIOM, Vienna, 18-19 October 1979, French, 46 pp.

The first part of this publication (La troisième révolution indus-trielle: microprocesseurs et robots, by Tom Stonier, Professor and President of the School of Science and Society, University of Bradford, U.K.) explains the main innovations within the techno-logical knowledge and its practical results, especially in the field of communication and information. The introduction of robots - for instance in the car industry - has changed the usual schemes of work conditions, union organizing and even social re-lationships. There are various attitudes concerning this problem: from the classic theory of "laissez-faire" to destructive tenden-cies which, as in the nineteenth century, are against any kind of "machines". The major difficulty is however the enormous power that multinational corporations have over production and techno-logical know-how. The author suggests various solutions such as a systematic decrease of hours of labour or the possibility given to workers to become skilled in different tasks so that they can be easily recycled. The multinationalization of trade unions seems to be necessary in view of the common effort to render the workers and the entire population ready to face this situation consciously.

The second document comes from the Ministry of Research and Tech-nology of the Federal Republic of Germany. It explains the new applications of electronic research and pinpoints through statis-tical data the industrial sectors which will be most affected.

A. Sivanandan, <u>Imperialism and Disorganic Development in the Silicon Age</u>, in: "Race and Class", London, 1979, English, 16 pp.

The technological revolution represented by the silicon chip, contains - as for every economic revolution - sharp contradictions within the capitalist processes and capability of renewing and developing itself. The economic structures follow an irregular pattern which divides the world of labour, thus creating unbalances and disorganic transformations. While in the centre (developed countries) the different aspects of capitalism have evolved gradually and organically, in the periphery (Third World) the capitalist mode of production has been grafted on the existing cultural and political order. This is why the revolutions in the periphery are not necessarily class based socialist revolutions and not even nationalist revolutions in the classic sense. They are mass movements with nationalist and revolutionary components, sometimes religious, sometimes secular, oftentimes both, but always against the repressive political state and its imperial backers.

<u>Problemi Internazionali</u> No. 19, FLM, Italy, August 1980, Italian, 79 pp.

This issue published by the Italian metalworkers federation offers an anthology of articles, documents and studies (many of which are reviewed in the original language) on the impact of the new technology, especially its implications for employment at the European level.

<u>Work and the Future</u>, a Report from the Industrial Committee of the General Synod Board for Social Responsibility, CIO Publishing, London, November 1979, English, 35 pp.

"The new technology holds out the promise of new jobs and of increased wealth... but in the short-term, a crisis faces our country." Starting from a Christian point of view this booklet analyzes technology, world development and jobs in the Eighties.

<u>The Impact of Microelectronics on the Third World: Problems and Potential</u>, from the book "Adjustment or Protectionism", edited by A.R. Riddell, CIIR, London, 1980, English, 20 pp.

"The flexible nature of the technology and the complex factors which will influence the rate and pattern of innovation and diffusion, make it difficult to predict the sectors most likely to be radically affected by the application of microelectronics even in the developed economies."

Paul Geelen, <u>How to Control New Technology and its Effects on Workers</u>, The Meeting, Milan, June 1980, English, 10 pp.

This paper presents a number of successful agreements and proposals made by workers of different industrial sectors and countries concerning the introduction of new technology: among others, the case of Lucas Aerospace, The Times (U.K.), the United Auto Workers (USA), the Algemene Bank Nederland (Holland), the Zendentsu (Telecommunications Workers Union in Japan), are illustrated.

Juan F. Rada, Microelectronics, information technology and its effects on developing countries, Pergamon Press, Oxford, 1979, English, 46 pp.

This study argues that current technological change in microelectronics (information technology) differs substantially from past innovations. This assessment is based on the facts that the nature of information technology relates to the extension and replacement of human intelligence functions, which in turn explain its pervasiveness; the speed of diffusion and transition from invention to innovation; the fact that it is scientifically and technologically based and affecting all sectors and, lastly, that it requires a world market for its economic exploitation.

Juan Rada, Some issues and possibilities posed by the Unfolding Information Revolution, Centre for Education in International Management, Geneva, February 1980, 50 pp.

The implication of microelectronics-based innovations in the discussion about a New International Order. The dynamism of scientific development conditions the development prospects of the South. A further polarization of international division of labour is not only possible but probable. Today we are faced with microelectronics, tomorrow bio-technology and on the horizon, the substitution of materials. These issues will change the very fabric of society.

Report on the 1979 World Conference on Faith, Science and the Future and Recommendations for Follow-up, from the Working Committee on Church and Society, WCC, June 1980, 35 pp.

Scientific knowledge as power and technology as its tool: power over people, over cultures and over nature. The search for a new definition of "appropriate technology" and "sustainable society". Ethical issues in the world energy debate. The ethical issues involved in the rapid emerging technologies of genetic modification (recombinant DNA technology). The use of new biotechnology in agriculture, microbial production processes and human genetics.

Jonathan King, Scientists in Society, document for the WCC Central Committee, Geneva, August 1980, 5 pp.

The new scientific revolutions in electronics with the growth of computers and in biology with the development of genetic engineering technology. The largest beneficiary and focus of this funding are for military and weapons research.

Alejandro Teitelbaum and Marcos Arruda, Notes on Transnational Corporations and Technology, a working paper for the Advisory Group on Economic Matters of the WCC, Rome, October 1980, 26 pp.

The impact of technology on human work, on the availability of jobs in the industrialized countries and in the underdeveloped countries, on work conditions, on the social organization of production, and on the food problem, the impact of farming technology and the transnational control of grain trade, and analysis of the Green Revolution. The role of corporations in the transfer of technology and the debate on codes of conduct.

The Lund monitor on Technological Trends and Challenges to the Third World, A Project Synopsis, by Hans Gustafson, Research Policy Studies, Lund University, Sweden, July 1980, 31 pp.

Introducing a new publication of the Research Policy Studies in the context of the "early warning system in technology and science for development": the LUND MONITOR, which will focus on micro-electronics and biotechnology.


Nora, Minc, Information de la société, Le Seuil, Paris, 1978

This study, commissioned by the French Government, is a worrying denunciation of the appropriation by the American data banks of what the authors call the "collective memory", i.e., a patrimony of information which cannot belong to private companies. The development of national information systems is one of the main guarantees of a country's independence and sovereignty.


## II.  THE DEVELOPMENT DEBATE

### 1. Basic Needs, People's Participation and the New International Economic Order

Emerging Trends in Development Theory, edited by Björn Hettne and Peter Wallensteen.  Available from SAREC, c/o SIDA, 105 25 Stockholm, Sweden.

Report on a Workshop on Development Theory held by the Swedish Agency for Research Cooperation with Developing Countries in August 1977.


Mecheline Rutjes, Basic-Needs Approach: a Survey of its Literature, Center for the Study of Education in Developing Countries (CESO-NUFFIC), The Hague, the Netherlands, April 1979, 20 pp.

An introduction to the basic-needs approach and strategy: its origin and the debate during the 1976 World Employment Conference. Survey of the literature published since then on this topic.


Patrick Healey, Basic Human Needs: The Politics of Mobilization, Department on Extension Studies, the University of Papua New Guinea, printed in Japan by the United Nations University, 1979, 21 pp.

The difference between the "growth oriented development model", the "employment oriented development model" and the "poverty eradication development model".  The emergence of the Basic Needs Approach and the attempts at a classification of the needs, people's participation and the mobilization of the disadvantaged both within poor nations, and of the poor nations confronting the rich is an essential requirement of a basic human needs approach to development.

Grundbedürfnisse/Grundbedürfnisstrategie, a bibliography prepared by the German Foundation for International Development in August 1979. Contains 118 articles and documents on the basic needs approach of development strategy. Available from: Endenicher-strasse 41, D-5300 Bonn, Federal Republic of Germany.


Peter R. Middelkoop, People's Participation in Development as a Basic Need, in "Exchange", Interuniversity Institute for Missio-logical and Ecumenical Research, Leiden, the Netherlands, December 1979, 30 pp.

The concept of "people's participation" in the thinking of the Commission on the Churches' Participation in Development of the WCC gradually led to the conceptualization of development as a struggle for social justice, self-reliance and economic growth. The author takes primary health care as an attempt at people's participation in development to meet a basic need.


Morris David Morris, Measuring the Condition of the World's Poor: The Physical Quality of Life Index, published for the Overseas Development Council by the Pergamon Policy Studies, 1717 Massa-chusetts Avenue N.W., Washington, D.C. 20036, USA, 1979, 178 pp.

The traditional yardstick of economic performance - per capita gross national product (GNP) - does not provide adequate informa-tion about the life chance of individuals in poor, or even rich, countries. The author introduces a new social indicator of development progress: the Physical Quality of Life Index (PQLI). A composite of life expectancy, infant mortality and literacy, the PQLI raises important questions that policymakers cannot ignore.


Preliminaries on a Comparative Analysis of the Various Viewpoints on the Quality of Life, the United Nations University, Tokyo, 1979, 45 pp.

An attempt at introducing a framework for a comparative analysis of the "quality of life" problématique - i.e., of the conceptual, methodological and operational aspects associated with this key issue of the contemporary debates focusing on societal develop-ment.


Michel Pagnier, Le nouvel ordre économique international, UNESCO, Paris, 1977, 29 pp.

A bibliography on the NIEO: origin and evolution of the concept; the main documents.


Letter to the First World from the Third World, Commission for Justice and Peace of Central America, November 1978, English, 18 pp.

At the end of the meeting of Roman Catholic laypersons, priests and bishops a series of letters were approved to send to the peoples of the industrialized countries. They contain statements

on the New International Economic Order, the multinational corporations in the Third World, and the role of Christians in the
struggle for justice.


Samuel L. Parmar, A Third World Perspective of the International
Economic Order and the Role of Transnationals, in ICCR Brief,
Interfaith Center on Corporate Responsibility, New York, January
1979, English, 4 pp.


For a NIEO, a dossier on the New International Economic Order prepared by the Commission on the Churches' Participation in Development of the World Council of Churches, Geneva, May 1979, 85 pp.

Contents - Some ecumenical views on the NIEO debate, Oaxtepec
          meeting, April 1979
        - Justice and Solidarity in the International Economic
          Order, by the Joint Conference of the Churches and
          Development in the Federal Republic of Germany
        - Statement on UNCTAD V, by the board of the Swiss
          Protestant Church Federation
        - Notes on NIEO, by Marcos Arruda
        - Report on the Current Position in the North-South
          Dialogue, by IDOC.


Backgrounders, issued by the Division for Economic and Social Information of the United Nations and available from the Non-governmental Liaison service of the UN both in New York and in Geneva,
1980.

A basic guide to North-South negotiaticns as they stand at the
beginning of the 1980s. Contents: a series of backgrounders on
the major economic and social issues confronting the international
community in 1980; a set of important resolutions adopted in recent years by the UN General Assembly; a booklet in question-
answer form containing basic material on the North-South dialogue,
negotiations and issues; a guide to the UN information system.


The Quest for Harmony: Perspectives on the New International
Development Strategy, a report of the Environment Liaison Centre,
Nairobi, Kenya, August 1980, 63 pp.

"The aim of this brief report is to support with facts and figures
the dissatisfaction of non-governmental organizations over the
development strategies pursued during the last 20 years." Content: general overview of development strategies and alternative
perspectives; world industrialization; feeding the world; energy
for food; tropical forests; energy and development; human settle-
ments; environmental economics.


Centre for Research on New International Economic Order (CRNIEO),
1 First St., Haddows Road, Madras 600 006, S. India.

This centre is based on the assumption that "the concerns represented by 'NIEO' embrace the totality of human life, seeking to
define and promote the quality of life of all sections of people

91

that inhabit the globe, humanization of modern technology as well
as responsible utilization and sharing of both natural and man-
made resources of the earth with all its inhabitants, present and
future." Since the establishment of a just society within a
country is a necessary corollary to the establishment of a NIEO,
the Centre has as objective to examine and define concepts of
development, for instance, the quality of life in the Indian cultural and well as Gandhian context, and to research the conditions
and the refractory factors of poverty and stagnation of the
weakest sections of the population in India.

The Third World Forum, c/o IFDA, 2 Place du Marché, CH-1260 Nyon,
Switzerland.

The Third World Forum is a network of social scientists and intel-
lectuals from the developing countries of Africa, Asia, Latin
America and the Middle East, who have a strong personal commitment
to the creation of a more just and equitable world. It seeks to
contribute to, and promote the development of, alternative conceptual frameworks for the analysis of problems faced by Third
World countries. By its composition, it reflects both the praxis
of the Third World struggle for liberation and the indispensable
intellectual development that can give content and direction to
that struggle.

## 2. Some Initiative Towards Alternative Patterns of Development and Life Styles

Maria Edy Chonchol, Guide bibliographique du Mozambique: Environ-
nement naturel, développement et organization villageoise, Ed.
L'Harmattan, Paris (16 rue des Ecoles, 75005 Paris), 1979,
French, 135 pp.

Mozambique as an attempt at implementation of "eco-development".
A basic bibliography on the development model and efforts in
Mozambique with particular reference to the preservation of the
natural environment and to the use of space.

Julius K. Nyerere, On Rural Development, ed. by the Food and Agriculture Organization of the United Nations, Rome, July 1979,
English, 15 pp.

President Nyerere's speech at the World Conference on Agrarian
Reform and Rural Development in Rome. Real development of a
nation - and of the whole world - has to go to the rural areas to
make life livable there by meeting basic needs. Conditions for
this are some very important political measures: land reform,
rural diversification, rural surplus used for rural betterment,
locally adapted technology, and people's active participation in
planning and decision making, i.e., "Power to the People."

Noël Givelet, The Fokonolona of Madagascar, in: IMCS Asia Document Reprint Service, 11/78, November 1978, English, 10 pp. (IDOC 32637).

Historical background, social and mythical roots of the grassroot socialism called Fokonolona in Madagascar, its re-awakening and reorganization through the Madagascar Revolution.

Rajni Kothari, Alternatives in Development - Perspective on Alternative Development Strategies for India, in: ICSSR Newsletter, Vol. IX, October 1978 - March 1979, Indian Council of Social Science Research, New Delhi, India, English, 14 pp. Alternatives in Development - Framework of Research, ibid., April-September 1979, 6 pp.

Attempt to spell out a broad framework of development strategies for our time, especially for a country like India. Three major aspects of development strategy: life styles (consensus on desirable and undesirable consumption standards, use and distribution of resources for the gratification of needs, norms for minima and maxima in incomes and wealth), organization of space (continuum of city, town and countryside with a production continuum of industry and agriculture), production system and technology (production and administration truly decentralized). Need for a re-thinking of education system; not specialists who are culturally illiterate and without a general analytical capacity for problem solving and creativity. Democratization of knowledge.

Education for Self-Reliance, by the Nordic Alternative Group, Helsinki, 1980, 36 pp.

The booklet is the result of a seminar held in summer 1979 in Cameroon. Its aim is to stress the conviction that emphasis on self-reliance should be integrated into all aspects of education.

Rethinking Development, proceedings of the World University Workshop held at the Sri Lanka Foundation Institute, Colombo, Sri Lanka, July 1978.

Discussion groups reports on life styles, transfer of technology, defence of human rights, development education, rural development and the new international economic order.

Another Development - Approaches and Strategies, the Dag Hammarskjöld Foundation, Övre Slottsgatan 2, S-752 20 Uppsala, Sweden.

A series of papers and reports elaborating the concepts outlined in, and continuing the discussion on, the 1975 Dag Hammarskjöld Project on Development and International Cooperation which led to the publication of What Now: Another Development.

Development Dialogue is the magazine of the Dag Hammarskjöld Centre (see address above), intended to provide a free forum for critical discussion of development priorities and problems and international development cooperation. The recent issues focus on:

- Another Development in Health, No. 1, 1978
- Another Development in Education, No. 2, 1978
- Towards Another Development in Science and Technology, No. 1, 1979
- Three Case Studies in Another Development, No. 2, 1979
- Another Development: Perspectives for the Eighties, No. 1, 1980
- The International Monetary System and the New International Order, No. 2, 1980.

## UNEP Seminars on Alternative Patterns of Development and Life-Styles

The United Nations Environment Programme (UNEP), in collaboration with the UN regional commissions, organized five continental seminars on alternative development patterns and life styles. It was part of the wider process being conducted by the United Nations of examining new paths of development in preparation for an international development strategy for the 1980s which the Special Session of the UN General Assembly tried to spell out in August 1980.

## 3. IFDA: The Search for Development Alternatives

The "International Foundation for Development Alternatives", Nyon, Switzerland, established on the initiative of individuals from both the Third World and some industrialized countries, tries to respond to needs for investigation and documentation of (a) innovative research, experimentation and action towards another development, and (b) of the full implications of the Only One Earth awareness in the North-South dialogue.

"Another development" to be explored as geared to the satisfaction of human needs on the basis of self-reliance and of harmony within the environment, as well as with the cultural and social values and aspirations of each society, whether in the industrialized countries or in the Third World.

IFDA Secretariat: 2 Place du Marché, CH-1260 Nyon, Switzerland.

## A United Nations Development Strategy for the 80s and Beyond - Participation of the "Third System" in its elaboration and implementation. A Project Description. Nyon, January 1978, English and French, 19+12 pp.

An analysis and description of working methods and organization necessary to implement the clearly defined needs of a New International Economic Order to which most people pay lip service, but which is shelved indefinitely because it is against the interests of the present power structures. An illustrative and tentative list of topics mention inter alia the problem of "de-linking" from the metropole and analysis of cases where this has been tried tentatively: Algeria, Burma, Chile, Cuba, Egypt, Iraq, Jamaica, Kampuchea, Madagascar, Peru, Somalia, Sri Lanka, Tanzania, Tunisia, Vietnam. Furthermore the possibilities of collective self-reliance.

For the industrialized nations, studies on new life styles, unemployment and new working types, free time, creative, non-market
oriented production, etc. Alternative export-import policies,
alternative energy resources, redistribution of wealth, income
gaps, restructuring of power and democratization of decision
making. Under "Third System", the study understand the "affected"
or "concerned themselves" over against the intergovernmental organizations (first system) and the transnational corporations
(second system).

Some of the most important articles published so far in the IFDA
Dossiers are:

P.B. Karandawela, Economic Cooperation Among Third World Countries:
The conceptual and institutional framework, in: IFDA Dossier 9,
July 1979, English 11 pp.

John Friedmann, Communalist Society: Some Principles for a Possible Future, in: IFDA Dossier 11, September 1979, English, 15 pp.

Socio-Cultural Investments Within the International Political
Economy of North-South Relations: The Role of Transnational Enterprises, by Karl P. Sauvant and Bernard Mennis, in: IFDA Dossier
12, October 1979, English, 14 pp.

Demain aujourd'hui: expérimentations sociales et changements de
styles de vie, by Michel Schiray and Silvia Sigal, in: IFDA
Dossier 15, December 1979, French, 11 pp.

Sovereignty of Needs, Reversal on Unjust Enrichment: Themes towards another development, by Prof. José R. Echeverria, in: IFDA
Dossier 15, January/February 1980, English, 11 pp.

Third World Commodity Policy at the Crossroads: Some Fundamental
Issues, by Carlos Fortin, in: IFDA Dossier 15, January/February
1980, English, 11 pp.

Ajit K. Ghose and Keith Griffin, Rural Poverty and Development
Alternatives in South and South-East Asia: Some Policy Issues,
in: IFDA Dossier 9, July 1979, English, 7 pp.

Development Alternatives - Some Canadian Signposts, by Cathy
Starrs, in: IFDA Dossier 12, October 1979, English, 14 pp.

The Strategy of Development in Eastern Europe, by Silviu Brucan
(Bucharest), in: IFDA Dossier 13, November 1979, English, 10 pp.

Local Action for Self-Reliant Development in Bangladesh, by Dr.
B.K. Jahangir, in: IFDA Dossier 15, January/February 1980,
English, 14 pp.

Another Development for Japan, by Nichikawa Jun, in: IFDA Dossier
15, January/February 1980, English, 15 pp.


4.  Ecodevelopment


The ecodevelopment approach was introduced during the 1972 environment conference in Stockholm.  It is now the object of research,
seminars and experimentation at the international and local levels.
Its basic aim is to harmonize the socio-economic objectives of
development with an ecologically sound and prudent management of
the resources and the environment.

Ecodevelopment is the basic intuition of the "International Research Center on Environment and Development" in Paris, established
with the support of the United Nations Environment Programme. Its
aim is to serve as a resource centre for researchers, change
agents and development workers. It publishes a quarterly entitled
Ecodevelopment News. Address: CIRED, 54 Boulevard Raspail,
Room 311, F-75270 Paris Cedex 06, France.

The founder and present director of CIRED, Ignacy Sachs, wrote a
book published in 1979, describing the basic assumptions behind
the ecodevelopment approach: Ignacy Sachs, Stratégies de l'éco-
développement, Editions économie et humanisme, éditions ouvrières,
Paris, 1979, 140 pp.

## III.  SOME PROBLEM AREAS: MOVEMENTS AND COUNTER-MOVEMENTS

### 1. The Threat of Death: Militarism and the Armaments Race

José-Antonio Viera Gallo, ed., The Security Trap - Arms Race,
Militarism and Disarmament: A Concern for Christians, IDOC-Inter-
national publication in collaboration with the CCIA of the World
Council of Churches, Rome, 1979, 266 pp.

Comprehensive tour d'horizon on arms race, its inner escalation
logics, militarism and the role of the churches in the disarmament
debate. Added is an ample bibliography of material available at
the IDOC Documentation Centre, Rome.

World Demilitarized: A Basic Human Need, by Demilitarization
Working Group of the World Order Models Project, Institute of
World Order, New York, USA, in: IFDA Dossier 11, September 1979,
English, 13 pp.

At this stage of international history the war system is global
in scope, encompassing in character, and dangerous in its implications for the future: it frustrates at the outset realistic policy
making for the elimination of misery, poverty, North-South inequality, violation of human rights, world population explosion,
pollution, etc.

Security, Disarmament and Economics - Socio-ethical challenges for
European churches and Christians after Helsinki and Belgrade,
Third post-Helsinki/Belgrade Consultation of the Conference of
European Churches, 26-29 September 1978, Siofok, Hungary, English
and French, 18 pp. (French: 21 pp.)

Group reports and recommendations on "Security through the arms
race?" with a call for "alternative security" and reflection on
the role of the churches. The signatories of the Helsinki Final
Act are responsible for 80% of the world's total expenditure on
armaments. Responsibility of the European churches.

Disarmament, Peace and Security, monthly bibliography of the UN
Geneva Unit Centre for Disarmament, Palais des Nations, Geneva,
English-French.

Militär, Militärhilfe, Rüstung, Abrüstung, Literaturhinweise zum Themenbereich Entwicklungspolitik/Entwicklungsländer, Nr. 34, Deutsche Stiftung für Internationale Entwicklung, Bonn (FRG), Spring 1978, 12 pp.

Over 80 entries, taken from the central documentation service of the German Foundation for International Development (DSE) on military matters, military aid, armament and disarmament.

World Armaments and Disarmament, SIPRI Yearbooks, Stockholm International Peace Research Institute, English.

A yearly report on the arms situation in the world: the international arms industry, arms traffic, arms race with detailed statistics.

Postures for Non-Proliferation - Arms Limitation and Security Policies to Minimize Nuclear Proliferation, SIPRI, Stockholm International Peace Research Institute, London, 1979, English, 168 pp.

The "injustices" inherent in the global SALT and Non Proliferation Treaty against the independence and security interests of smaller non-nuclear states can be outbalanced only by new forms of drastic disarmament measures by the super-powers.

Strategic Survey 1978, by The International Institute for Strategic Studies (IISS), London, 1979, English, 142 pp.

The international military scene, analysis of the USA-USSR military balance, new factors in the arms race. The assessment is made from a Western point of view and inclined to portray a military superiority and threat of the USSR.

Disarmament, Development, and a Just World Order, ed. by Centre for the Study of Developing Societies, Delhi, 1978, English, 106 pp. (+ Declaration). (IDOC 33743)

Papers submitted to an International Workshop on Disarmament in Delhi, March 1978. Among specifics of the nuclear threat and the arms race, topics like "International Power Structures and Developing Countries," "Non-Alignment in a Nuclear Weapons Culture," arms trade and disarmament were discussed.

Erklärung "Sicherung des Friedens" contra Aktion "Ohne Rüstung leben" - Protestanten für und gegen Militär, in: epd-Documentation, Nr. 40a/80, 5 September 1980, German, 12 pp.

Well-known protestant Christians have signed a statement in defence of the right of a state to protect its safety if necessary also by weapons, and have questioned the fundamental assumptions of the movement "Ohne Rüstung leben" (to live without armaments). This issue of epd contains the former statement, a statement of "Ohne Rüstung leben," statements of churches.

Spezieller Wahnsinn: Mittelstreckenraketen in Europa - Ein Kapital
europäischer Selbstachtung, IDOC-MINI-Pamphlet, 1980, German,
64 pp.

The decision of NATO for the euromissiles is seen in the absurd
logic of militarism and military industry. In the socialist bloc
and in the so-called "free world" the same mechanisms of fear and
"we cannot otherwise" are used to justify the arms race. The euromissiles are good in creating some more first class targets for
Soviet weapons, they change the euro-strategic balance in favour
of NATO, they endanger readiness for SALT III (on medium range
systems), their installation will be politically disastrous (cold
war renewal) and force all sides into an escalated arms race.


Erklärung zur gegenwärtigen weltpolitischen Situation, Bund der
Evangelischen Kirchen in der Deutschen Demokratischen Republik,
Berlin, 22 January 1980, German, 4 pp.

This declaration of the Protestant Churches in the DDR warns
against arms race in the world, and against the euromissiles, and
supports the WCC programme against militarism.


Rocco Baione, Corsa agli armamenti e disarmo in recenti pronun-
ciamenti della chiesa, in: Aggiornamenti sociali, XXXI/2 February
1980, Italian, 19 pp.

The recent threats to world peace are commented in the light of
well-known Roman Catholic teachings: the Council of Vatican II on
the immorality of the arms race, the various allocutions of Paul
VI, also before the UN General Assembly, his encyclical letter
"Populorum Progressio", etc. The present Pope, John Paul II, has
continued in this line. The NATO decision on euromissiles has
met with clear opposition from the Pope (Allocution to Cardinals,
22 December 1979); the menace of an atomic global holocaust was
conjured in the Pope's New Year's homily. The underlying link of
hunger and misery and the inhuman arms race and its costs have
been accused by John Paul II in his message in the UN General
Assembly, 2 October 1979, in his allocution to the Diplomatic
Corps (14 January 1980), and in his encyclical letter "Redemptor
Hominis" (No. 16).


The Programme on Militarism and Armaments Race, World Council of
Churches, Central Committee, Kingston, Jamaica, 1-11 January 1979,
CCIA Related Matters, Geneva 1979, 12 pp.

The WCC paper analyzes the all-pervading militarism in social and
political life through the brain-washing by "National Security"
ideology, the qualitative alteration of militarism today by the
capacity of global reach and overkill potential. Part iii. outlines an Action/Reflection Programme for the churches.


Militarism and the World Military Order, A Study Guide for the
Churches, by Ernie Regehr, Commission of the Churches on International Affairs, WCC, Geneva, 1980, 69 pp.

A booklet introducing the issue of militarism: its dynamics (arms
race and arms trade), its fruits (insecurity, human rights

98

violations and underdevelopment), its roots (factors contributing to militarism).


L'arme de la non-violence, in: Témoignage chrétien, No. 1 859, 25 February - 3 March, 1980, French, 4 pp.

Non-violent movements like Centre de formation et de recherche pour une autre défense, Communauté de l'Arche, Mouvement international de la Réconciliation, Mouvement pour une Alternative non-violente, etc., try to conscientize people on new forms of non-violent civil defence. It is a new life style with a new ethics of lived communalism and the awareness for all living beings, now and in future. Necessity of political option and action.


## 2. The Nuclear Debate

Anna Gyorgy and Friends, No Nukes: Everyone's Guide to Nuclear Power, South End Press, Box 68 Astor Station, Boston, Massachusetts 02123, 1979.

"No Nukes" is a comprehensive guide to nuclear power which explains the inner workings of nuclear plants, the nuclear fuel cycle, nuclear health and safety hazards, the economics and politics of nuclear power, and the activities of citizen groups around the world. The authors detail the history of the nuclear programme, and describe the impact that Nukes can have on jobs, taxes, and the community. The book also introduces readers to wind, solar, geothermal, tidal, fossil fuel, and conservation alternatives through a discussion of their political implications and economic costs.


Nuclear Energy and Nuclear Weapon Proliferation, SIPRI (Stockholm International Peace Research Institute), London, 1979, English, 462 pp.

Papers and discussions of an international conference of experts, sponsored by SIPRI, at Stockholm, October 1978, on the technical aspects of the control of fissionable materials in non-military applications.


Green Evolution, Vol. 36, No. 5, Mid-Summer, 1979, USA, English, 40 pp.

A special Nuclear Education Issue of the Green Evolution magazine. The situation of US nuclear energy programme, the various dangers, contradictions, official fallacious propaganda, ethical issue, anti-nuclear action groups.


Counter Information Services, Anti-Report No. 22 (CIS, 9 Poland Street, London Wl), undated, English 40 + cover pp.

This issue is part of the Transnational Institute programme on the international nuclear industry. It looks behind the interests of the British nuclear establishment by business, multis, politicians.

The problems of the fuel cycle (waste) and the safety issue. Appendix with glossary, reactor types, nuclear consortia.

Nuclear Power, by Issue (The United Church of Canada), April 1977, reprinted September 1978, English, 10 (newspaper size) pp.

Introduction into the nuclear energy problématique, explanation of key concepts. Review of books and articles on the subject, addresses of Canadian resource organizations.

Who's On First? What's on Second? - A Grassroot Political Perspective on the Anti-Nuclear Movement, by Marty Jezer, in: WIN, October 12, 1978, English, 12 pp.

The article attempts to analyze non-violent direct action within a more political grassroots perspective, after the ban-the-bomb, civil rights and anti-war movements. A new analytical and political approach is necessary to widen public support.

Marketing the Nuclear Nightmare - Profiles of US Exports to Five Countries, by NARMIC (National Action/Research on the Military Industrial Complex), a Project of the American Friends Service Committee, 1501 Cherry Street, Philadelphia, Pennsylvania 19102, December 1979, English, 8 pp.

Brief information on the US nuclear deal with Brazil and Argentina, South Africa, South Korea, the Philippines. Addresses of resource organizations.

500 Mile Island: The Philippine Nuclear Reactor Deal, by Walden Bello, Peter Hays and Lyuba Zarsky, Pacific Research, First Quarter, 1979, 45 pp.

"The political and economic fall-out from the nuclear accident at Three Mile Island, Pennsylvania, has created a political climate in which new US reactor construction will be severely curtailed, at least in the short run. But the American nuclear industry is far from dead. Nuclear expansion continues in other parts of the world, particularly where political opposition is suppressed." With these words, the Pacific Studies Center opens its fine report on the international links in the nuclear "chain". It demonstrates how the growth of opposition to nuclear power in the developed countries has stepped up nuclear expansion in the Third World, where reactor exports pose even graver safety and environmental hazards. The first two articles examine the particularly perilous bargain between the Marcos government and Westinghouse to build a nuclear reactor on the Bataan Peninsula, supported by huge sums from the US Export-Import Bank. "In the Philippines, just as in the US or Australia, energy is a question of political power, not merely technology... In uniting across national boundaries," the report concludes: "the anti-nuclear movement... must address political issues, such as Martial Law in the Philippines." (From ISIS International Bulletin, No. 15, p. 35).

Congress against the Nuclear Cooperation between FRG and SA, Bonn, 11/12 November 1978 - Documentation; ed. by Anti-Apartheid Bewegung in the Federal Republic of Germany, Bonn, December 1979, English, 40 pp.

Material proving the long collaboration between German technology and industry with the silent permission of the Federal government and the South African nuclear programme.

Das deutsch-brasilianische Bombengeschäft, special issue of "Lateinamerika Nachrichten," Berlin (West), 1980, 159 pp. DM 7.

Analysis, documents and reports on German-Brazilian collaboration in the nuclear field, focussing on the social and economic consequences for Brazil. (LN, Savignyplatz 5, D-1000 Berlin 12).

## 3. Multinational Corporations

Research on multinational corporations greatly expanded in the last few years. The following are some of the organizations specializing in data gathering on this issue.

### Corporate Data Exchange (CDE)

This group produces various publications which are primarily data oriented consisting of directories and handbooks or specific studies. Up to now CDE has produced directories on agribusiness, on transportation, on energy, and on banking and finances, and handbooks on US bank loans to South Africa and pension fund investments. Address: 193 Broadway, Room 706-7, New York, N.Y. 10038, USA.

### ILET (Instituto Latinoamericano de Estudios Transnacionales)

It is an independent research institute studying the impact of transnational corporations on Latin American and Third World countries. Its studies are often based on a sociological approach and investigate the nature of the prevailing power structure. The work is organized through a series of projects of publications. Address: Apartado 35-025, Mexico 20, DF, Mexico.

### SOMO

This group collects financial information on 500 multinationals based in Europe and Japan. Much of the information is based on clippings from 100 business and financial journals. The work is divided into four sections: specific corporations, branches of industry, country files, organizations. Address: Paulus Potterstraat 20, Amsterdam, Netherlands.

The Asia/North America Communications Center (A/NACC), in Hong Kong, has built up an impressive data base on the activities of multinational corporations in Asia. It publishes a quarterly magazine Asia Monitor, covering trends and development in each

country of Asia. In 1979, A/NACC published America in Asia,
Vol. 1, a research guide on U.S. economic activitiy in Asia.
A/NACC also has a special project on "Occupational Safety and
Health in Asia's Chemical Processing Industry". Starting in
1980, it launched a research and publication project on the U.S.
military presence in Asia. Address: 2 Man Wan Rd. 17-C,
Kowloon, Hong Kong.


## CETRAL (Centre de Recherche sur l'Amérique Latine et le Tiers Monde)

This group, based at the Paris University, is formed of re-
searchers of the faculty of Sociology under the direction of
Gonzalo Arroyo. Till now they have published a series of
dossiers on agribusiness and agriculture in the following Latin
American countries: Honduras, Argentina, Brazil, Colombia and
Venezuela. Address: 35 rue des Jeûneurs, F-75002 Paris, France.


## TIE (Transnational Information Exchange)

Born in 1978, TIE is a network of European-based groups re-
searching on TNCs and their impact on employment, labour conditions, future trends in Europe as well as in the Third World.
They produce a quarterly magazine called "TIE Bulletin" of documentation and information on TNCs (first issues dealing with car
industry). As part of the network IDOC functions as documentation centre on the following sectors: agribusiness, car industry
and its connections with the armaments industry, and electronics
industry in the perspective of the new technology. Address of
"TIE-Bulletin": c/o Transnational Institute, Paulus Potterstraat
20, Amsterdam, Netherlands; for documentation: IDOC International,
Via Santa Maria dell'Anima 30, 00186 Rome, Italy.


## Data Center

This centre consists of a library whose aim is that of reflecting
the struggle between capital and labour. It provides also information services on major corporations, banks, industries, and
the struggle to resist these dominant forces of capitalism by
labour and liberation movements. Address: 464 19th Street,
Oakland, California 94612, USA.


## "Multinational Monitor"

It is a new monthly magazine sponsored by Ralph Nader's organization in the USA. It provides critical discussion of the role of
multinational enterprises in Third World development. Well-known
journalists contribute to it. Address: P.O. Box 19312,
Washington, D.C. 20036, USA.


## UN Centre on Transnational Corporations

It is an autonomous body within the UN whose objectives are to
further the understanding of the nature of TNCs and of their
political, legal, economic and social effects on home and host

countries and to strengthen the capacity of developing countries
in their dealings with TNCs. Aside from specialized researches
this centre publishes a regular magazine "The CTC Reporter".
Address: United Nations, New York, USA.


4. Environment Movements


Aktionen der Ökologisbewegung dokumentiert und reflektiert, in:
Gewaltfreie Aktion, Vol. 10, 1. u. 2. Quartal 1978, German, 88 pp.

Various anti-nuclear action programmes: the tactics and juridical
implications of the household electricity bill boycott action;
the intervention in shareholders assemblies of electricity companies; the mobilization and activities of workers committees
for the objectives of the ecomovement; examples: Lucas Aerospace,
Chrysler, the Green Ban Group. While the first two examples are
taken from the Federal Republic of Germany, the third from the UK,
another article speaks about the anti-nuclear movement in
Australia. Finally an article on ecology movements in the Third
World. Other articles speak about the connection between ecology
and disarmament.


Aufbruch in eine bssere Zukunft – Die Grünen und ihre Abkehr vom
Prinzip des unbegrenzten Konsums, in: Der Spiegel, Nr. 13/80,
24 March 1980, German, 12 pp.

The weak common denominator of the various trends within the
"Green Party", political spearhead of the various ecomovements
and "Bürgerinitiativen" in the FRG. Their chance is the insen-
sitivity of the established parties for urgent ecological, energy,
participatory issues and their incapacity to take controversial,
unpopular or anti-lobby measures. The political trend among the
18-30 year-old Germans and the relatively bigger appeal of ecological issues among this group.


Ecologie – des mouvements en mouvement, issue of La Revue
Nouvelle, 10 October 1978, French, 198 pp.

Whole issue dedicated to the eco-movement, main ecology movements
and action programmes in Belgium; some small contributions on
"Why ecology"; ecology and politics.


Celeste Wesson, Eco-Feminism, in: "Win", USA, 1 March 1980.

Presentation of a Conference on "Women and Life on Earth: Eco-
Feminism in the 80s" held March 21-23, 1980, in Amherst, Massachusetts, USA. For information: P.O. Box 580, Amherst, Massachusetts 01002, USA.


Bernard Charbonneau, Feu vert, auto-critique du mouvement éco-
logique, Editions Karthala, 22-24 Boulevard Arago, F-75013 Paris,
1980, 208 pp.

B. Charbonneau, who took active part in the emergence and organization of the environment movement in France during the last

50 years, writes both the history and self-criticism of this movement and proposes the main lines of an ecological policy which could transform a spontaneous movement into a powerful political alternative.

Marlène Tuininga, La Vie autrement - Ecologie et non-violence aujourd'hui, in: Informations Catholiques Internationales, No. 523, 15 February 1978, French, 10 pp.
Background on the historical, sociological, political issues of the ecomovement in general, and particularly in France. Its objectives in the global context "Only One Earth", i.e., dilemmas facing industrialized and Third World nations alike, non-violence, anti-militarism and anti-nuclear connections. Role of the institutional church. But on the grassroot level, through M.L. King, Gandhi, César Chavez, there is a continuity with primordial Christian thinking, rather "hoping".

Reimer Gronemeyer, The Development of a New Political Culture, manuscript, UN University, Switzerland, April 1978, English, 10 pp.
Industrialization and high technology is destroying the natural resources in the First and Third World. A new culture must be the strict opposite of the one-dimensional world culture of industrial dictate: a culture of living differently. Values are beauty, life, self-reliance, self-determination (decentralization), creativity.

A Theology of Ecology, prepared by the Task Force on Christian Life Style and Ecology of the Christian Church (Disciples of Christ), and published in Social Action Newsletter, Indianapolis, USA, Spring 1980. It can be obtained from the Department of Church in Society, P.O. Box 1986, Indianapolis, Indiana 46206, USA.

5. The Women's Movement

Barbara Rogers, The Domestication of Women: Discrimination in Developing Societies, Kogan Page, London, 1980, 200 pp.
This study is primarily about women and how development planners relate to them. The author assesses the discriminatory impact of Western culture and poverty on poor women in the Third World in the process of what the Western world calls development.

Let me Speak! Testimony of Domitila, a woman of the Bolivian Mines, by Domitila Barrios de Chungara with Moema Viezzer, Monthly Review Press, 1978, USA, 234 pp.
The story of a woman of the Bolivian Andes, wife of a tin miner, mother of seven children, militant women's leader from Catavi. It is a living testimony and a first-hand account from a woman's viewpoint of the continuing confrontations between the miners and the government over the last fifteen years.

No Time for Crying, a dossier available from the Resource Center for Philippine Concerns, P.O. Box 2784, Kowloon Central Post Office, Hong Kong, 1980.

A dossier of testimonies by Filipina women about their lives and struggles in a country suffering from an oppressive, martial law regime.


Sara Evans, Personal Politics, Alfred A. Knopf, Publc., New York, 1979, 274 pp.

The subtitle is: the roots of women's liberation in the civil rights movement and the new left.


Human Rights, World Council of Churches, Geneva, 1979.

A collection of articles, in loose-leaf pull-out form focussing on women and human rights. It is a selection of papers presented at the conference on Human Rights in Vienna, June 1979, organized by the women's desk of the World Council of Churches. Subjects covered include: sexism and racism, battered women, prostitution in the Philippines and Japan, violations of human rights of women and children in Latin America (Argentina, Chile and Uruguay), women in prison, migrant workers in Australia, and specific situations in Ghana, Brazil and Chile.


Julia Baliot, Zur besonderen Lage der Frau in Südafrika, in: "blätter des iz3w", March 1979, German, 5 pp.

A documented insight into the daily siuation of suffering and humiliation of women under the apartheid racism.


Namibian Women and their role in SWAPO's struggle, paper presented by SWAPO Women's Council at the International Conference in Solidarity with the Struggle of the People of Namibia, Paris, September 1980, English, 6 pp.

Social and political dimension of women's liberation in Namibia.


ISIS, Women's International Information and Communication Service, Via della Pellicia 31, 00153 Rome, Italy; Case Postale 301, CH-1227 Carouge/Geneva, Switzerland.

ISIS is a resource and documentation centre in the international women's movement. It was set up in 1974 by a collective of women to gather materials from local women's groups and the feminist movement, particularly in the developing world, and to make these resources available to other women. The quarterly ISIS International Bulletin reproduces theoretical and practical information and documentation from women's groups and the women's movement around the world. ISIS recently started a Spanish edition of their Bulletin. Recent ISIS International Bulletins:

No. 7 and 8, Women and Health, 1978
No. 9, Women in Southern Africa, 1978
No. 10, Women Workers, 1978/1979
No. 11, Women, Land and Food Production, 1979

No. 12, <u>Organizing Against Rape</u>, 1979
No. 13, <u>Tourism and Prostitution</u> in S.E. Asia, 1979
No. 14, <u>Migrant Women</u>, 1980
Spanish edition: <u>Mujer: Problemas y Perspectivas</u>, December 1979
<u>Mujeres y Salud</u>, April 1980
Forthcoming (1980): a Resource Guide on Women and Development


## 6. Ethnic Minorities and Indigenous Peoples

<u>Identity and Justice - Report of an Ad Hoc Meeting on Race and Minority Issues in Asia</u>, ed. by Urban Rural Mission - Christian Conference of Asia, Hong Kong, 1977, English, 64 pp.

Reports from oppressed minorities and their situation in Australia, the Philippines, Japan, India, New Zealand.

<u>Christian Response to Race and Minority Issues in Asia</u>

Proceedings and findings of a regional consultation organized by the Christian Conference of Asia in cooperation with the World Council of Churches, New Delhi, 24-29 March 1980.

<u>Land Rights and Racially Oppressed Indigenous People</u>, WCC Programme Unit on Justice and Service, Committee Meeting, Kingston, Jamaica, January 1-11, 1979, English, 17 pp.

The battle between colonizing powers and the pushing back of indigenous people; two case studies: Australia and Brazil. Denying of land rights to indigenous people is always concomitant with racialist discrimination, and has its basis in economic exploitation, nowadays by the transnational corporations. Short bibliography.

Hugh and Karmel McCullum, <u>This Land is not for Sale</u>, Anglican Bookcentre, Toronto, Canada, 1975, English, 213 pp.

This book is about Indian, Inuit and Metis land claims and northern development in Canada. It is about energy, government and the church... about industrialists and businessmen who use Canada's colonial approach to the North for multinational profiteering.

A. Barrie Pittock, <u>Australian Aborigines: The Common Struggle for Humanity</u>, IWGIA Document 39, International Work Group for Indigenous Affairs, Copenhagen, 1979, English, 40 pp. Spanish résumé and translation, 18 pp.

Historical Background of the Australian "Native question", their political rights, the mining rights and exploitations of the aborigines.

The Aborigines Today: Land Rights, Uranium mining, social disruption, in: "Survival International Review", Summer 1978, United Kingdom, English, 25 pp.

Special issue on problems facing the aborigines in Australia, their repression by economic interests, especially of transnational corporations like Rio Tinto Zinc, busy in the uranium mining industry.

Gottfried Deelen, Brasilianische Landwirtschaft bietet keinen Platz für Kleinbauern-Entwicklung und Unterentwicklung in der brasilianischen Landwirtschaft, manuscript, 1979 (?), German, 27 pp. (IDOC 32580)

The development policy, oriented towards national prestige, gives priority to the bigger agricultural enterprises at the expense of small land owners and the proletarization of the agricultural labourers. These "boias frias" without regular work have no membership rights in trade unions. The most fatal consequences for Indians and peasants of this government policy and the exploitation of land by the international and national agribusiness firms occurs in the Amazonas. Role of the Churches and the basic communities.

## Historical Background on the Chico Dam Controversy

A mimeographed article that provides ample historical documentation on the growing opposition of the Kalinga people (Philippines) to the building of dams in their area. It is condensed from The Chico River Basin Development Project: A Case Study in National Development, a paper presented at the 3rd National Annual Conference of the Anthropological Association of the Philippines, 22-27 April 1980.

Squatters in Their Own Land, by Ben and Nilo Langa-an, provides comprehensive treatment of the problems of non-Muslim cultural minorities in the Philippines. Printed in Manila, May 1980, the book contends that the minority problem is only one aspect of a grave national crisis that draws the country ever closer to a revolutionary war; 143 pp.

## Organizations dealing with minority rights:

| | |
|---|---|
| Urban Rural Mission - Christian Conference of Asia | 2-3-18 Nishi-Waseda, Shinjuku-ku, Tokyo 160, Japan |
| Minority Rights Group | Benjamin Franklin House, 36 Craven Street, London WC2N 5NG, Great Britain |
| Survival International | 36 Craven Street, London WC2N 5NG, Great Britain |
| International Work Group for Indigenous Affairs (IWGIA) (publishes IWGIA Document series and IWGIA Newsletter) | Frederiksholms Kanal 4A DK-1220 Copenhagen K, Denmark |

| | |
|---|---|
| American Indian Movement | c/o Vernon Bellancourt,<br>P.O. Box 190,<br>Minneapolis, Minnesota 55440, USA |
| Project North/Plan Nordique<br>Interchurch Project on<br>Northern Development<br>(Publishes a Newsletter) | 154 Glenrose Avenue,<br>Toronto, Ontario M4T 1K8,<br>Canada |
| Colonial and Indigenous<br>Minorities Research and<br>Action (CIMRA) | 92 Plimsoll Road, London N4,<br>Great Britain. |

## 7. Consumer Action

The International Organization for Consumers Unions links the
activities of consumer organizations in some 50 countries. An
independent, non-profit making and non-political foundation,
IOCU promotes world-wide cooperation in consumer protection,
education and information and the comparative testing of consumer goods and services. Address: IOCU, 9 Emmastraat,
NL-2595 EG The Hague, Netherlands.

The IOCU Regional Office for Asia and the Pacific, based in
Penang, Malaysia, published in January 1980 a booklet called
Consumer Action in Developing Countries. The 63-page booklet
deals with such varied topics as drugs and double standards, the
relevance of consumer movements to less developed countries, and
sweetened condensed milk. It is the first of a series called
Consumercraft which is designed to

- provide an insight into consumer problems,
- record experiences of consumer groups, particularly in
  developing countries,
- share ideas and frameworks for action with new organizations
  in developing countries.

The Consumer Action Charter pinpoints five principles as the
basis for consumer actions and campaigns:

- critical awareness
- involvement or action
- social responsibility
- ecological responsibility
- solidarity

Address: P.O. Box 1045, Penang, Malaysia.

## Periodicals of Public Interest Organizations/A Citizen's Guide

This booklet, prepared by the Commission for the Advancement of
Public Interest Organizations lists 96 organizations and 103
periodicals of citizen action, in the field of health, housing,
taxes, agriculture and food policies, energy, natural resources,
foreign and military policy, civil liberties, self-reliance,
community change, consumer access, telecommunications, appropriate technology, corporate accountability, etc., in the United

States. The directory can be ordered from: the Commission for the Advancement of Public Interest Organizations, 1875 Connecticut Avenue, NW 1013, Washington, D.C. 20009, USA.

IOC-MAB - International Meeting Center of Grassroots Movements Kuringersteenweg 35, B-3500 Hasselt, Belgium.
A centre open to all people working with the grassroots for political alternatives and new life styles and promoting an exchange of experiences and insights at the international level. Includes groups and movements both in the industrialized countries and in the Third World. Publishes a quarterly bulletin.

Poor People's Movements, by Frances Fox Piven and Richard A. Cloward, Vintage Books, New York, 1979, 381 pp.
A history of spontaneous movements of poor people in the USA. Why protest struggles succeed or fail.

IV. TOWARDS A NEW ETHICS - NEW LIFE STYLES AND THE CHURCHES

The Emergence of a New Ethics

Valentina Borremans, Reference Guide to Convivial Tools, draft, 1978, Cuernavaca, Mexico, 320 pp.
A bibliography on user-value oriented modern tools, based on more than fifteen years of documentation work at the CIDOC centre in Cuernavaca. The resource guide deals with such issues as radical technologies, environment problems and movements, new communities and new life styles. The underlying value is conviviality.

Taking Charge, by the Simple Living Collective, American Friends Service Committee, San Francisco, Bantam Books, 1977, 341 pp.
This book is about taking charge of our lives by living simply. But much more important is the impact that this can have on the global environment and on the oppressed of the world. Two-thirds of the pages are devoted to practical suggestions, simple and creative activities which can be done with families and friends and build alternatives.

Demain aujourd'hui: expérimentation sociale, changements de styles de vie et de développement, Centre international de recherche sur l'environnement et le développement (CIRED), Paris, 1978, French, 61 pp.
Presentation of a research project on alternative development and new life styles. Description of the aims and programme of CIRED (see above: "ecodevelopment").

Campaign for Human Redevelopment, Los Angeles Catholic Worker Movement, "Catholic Agitator", Los Angeles, November 1978.

Presentation of a programme for "human redevelopment": "clearly, the single most important force facing those who work with the inner-city poor is redevelopment."


Alternativ Bewegung, Neuer Lebensstil und Entwicklung, Evangelische Pressedienst, Frankfurt, "epd-Entwicklungspolitik", July 1979.

A bibliography on alternative movements, new life styles and development.


Choosing Life in an End Time, "Catholic Agitator", Los Angeles, March 1979, 16 pp.

How to practise hope, celebrate life and wage the struggle while public policies are preparing for doomsday (especially the re-armament mood). An ethic for an end time.


Beyond Simple Living: Community, Alliances and Action, in: "Win", USA, 12 July 1979.

The simple living movement will be successful only if it is accompanied by an awareness of oppression and liberation, by a political strategy for change and by the search for alliances in action.


Ehrhard Eppler, Anfragen an unseren Lebensstil, in epd-Entwicklungspolitik, April 1979, German, 9 pp.

Nobody may advocate change in the unjust North-South relationship if he is not ready to fight inequality and unjust power structures within either North or South themselves. Economic and political democracy and participation need a new life style, not as a "less", but as more intensity of living, instead of passive consumerism and comfort.


The Cultural Roots of Another Development, by Rajni Kothari, in: IFDA Dossier 12, October 1979, English, 12 pp.

The quest for an alternative development is basically a question of values and ethical options. The dilemma of the "philosophy of modernity" (the end of life is indefinite economic prosperity in the service of which all inanimate resources are consumed and animate resources of the biosphere are sacrificed) has been obvious in the fatal divisions of the world (colony-colonized, metropole-periphery, urban-rural, racial, ideological, sex roles...). A new holistic approach has to be one of empathy and solidarity, philosophically one which undoes the mortiferous marriage between science and technology (knowledge as servant of productivity only), in which knowledge became the mere know-how of power. Earlier systems of wisdom in mankind (Buddhist, Hindu, Zoroaster, Islam) have to be re-evaluated.

Joseph B. Board, Only Human: The Quality of Life Debate in Sweden, in: Current Sweden, No. 242, January 1980, English, 8 pp.

Sweden seen as a microcosmic example of causes and effects in a capitalist-socialist welfare state that touch the entire Western world. The Swedish "cultural debate" over the modernization backlash. End of the materialist ethos, search for individuality, individual responsibility (individual in contrast to institutional), individual compassion, creativity, spontaneous human relationships, human relationship to nature and neighbourhood, holistic view of the components for satisfying human needs. Résumé of a series of articles in Svenska Dagbladet: leitmotiv of the 1980 politics should be to counteract psychic impoverishment, the values "create, let-live, and stimulate to action" in contrast to "govern, bureaucratize, and level", to encourage spontaneous grassroots groups. Sweden has an Institute for Social Research, created by Parliamentary Act in 1974, headed by Sten Johansson.


Harlan Cleveland and Thomas W. Wilson, Humangrowth - An Essay on Growth Values and the Quality of Life, Aspen Institute Publications, 360 Bryant Street, P.O. Box 1652, Palo Alto, California 94302, USA.

The "growth ethic" and the need to set new goals for growth.


Into the 1980s: Some Ecumenical Views on the Challenges to Values and Structures, CCPD-WCC Advisory Group on Economic Matters, Le Cénacle, Geneva, 10-14 January 1980.

Given the current crisis of the international system born after World War II, there is a need for a new paradigm in political economy. The report underlines some signs of the times marking the setting of the 1980s: the new role of the poor, the Islamic resurgence, human rights and the struggle against repression, rise of a new conservatism. It then lists three scenarios or visions of the future: continuation and reinforcement of the existing order, organizing for change around long-term, complementary self-interests; toward a just, participatory and sustainable society. In order to achieve the third scenario, some changes are needed both at the national level (in the Third World and in the industrialized countries) and at the international level. In developing countries, structural changes should lead towards self-reliance and interdependence. In the industrialized countries, the 1970s witnessed the emergence of new values challenging the idea of progress and stressing humanization. "Our final concern in the 1980s should be to keep human life human under the stresses and opportunities of economic growth. Such a strategy for development should yield positive results in the lives of people whom, in moving poetry, Rabindranath Tagore has identified as the poorest, the lowliest, the exploited, and the lost."

## The Role of the Churches

New Life Styles, SODEPAX, Geneva, 3 October 1977

Report of Group V of SODEPAX meeting in 1977: the call to simplicity of life and concern for the poor as depicted in the Bible;
the values of solidarity and sharing today; the search for a new
world order: concrete elements could be worked out on an analysis
of the needs of people and on the affirmation of corresponding
rights for all humankind.


Convergence for Justice, statement by the Leadership Conference
of Women Religious and the Conference of Major Superiors of Men
in the USA, Cleveland, Ohio, 27 August - 1 September 1978.

Commitment of R. Catholic religious towards solidarity with the
poor and the oppressed, simpler life styles and struggle for
social justice.


William E. Gibson, A Covenant Group for Lifestyles Assessment,
United Presbyterian Church, USA, 1978, 111 pp.

A programme of life styles assessment for small groups - 7 to 14
adults - in 12 sessions of approximately 2 1/2 hours. Addressed
to "rich Christians" this programme considers life styles options
in response to a) the hunger/ecology/justice crisis and b) the
freedom and responsibility given by the Gospel. The document
contains a good definition, description and analysis of life
styles and the change process resulting from global awareness.


Beyond Survival: Bread and Justice in Christian Perspective,
Dieter T. Hessel, ed. Friendship Press, New York, 1977.

Chapter 6, The Lifestyle of Christian Faithfulness, is the product of a theological-ethical study team under the guidance of
William E. Gibson.


UNCTAD V and the People: A Christian Statement, by the Ecumenical
Secretariat for UNCTAD V (members: the National Council of
Churches in the Philippines, the Association of Major Religious
of Men and Women in the Philippines, the National Secretariat for
Social Action, Justice and Peace of the Catholic Bishops' Con-
ference of the Philippines, and the Office for Human Development
of the Federation of Asian Bishops' Conference), Manila, May 1979,
English, 5 pp.

International conferences such as UNCTAD V have a meaning only if
they benefit the poor and contribute to a change in world and
national structures towards self-reliance and democracy.


Justice and Solidarity in the International Economic Order,
Gemeinsame Konferenz der Kirchen für Entwicklungsfragen, Federal
Republic of Germany, 21 February 1979, available in German,
French, Spanish and English.

Declaration of the Joint Conference of the Churches on Development
(made of the Association of the Protestant Churches' Development
Services and the Catholic Commission for Justice and Peace) in
the Federal Republic of Germany on the occasion of UNCTAD V.

Vincent Cosmao, L'Eglise dans la Crise mondiale, Réflexions
après la CNUCED V, "Foi et Développement", Centre Lebret, Paris,
June-July 1979, French, 4 pp.

Reflections following UNCTAD V. The present crisis is a challenge
for the churches. Contribution to the North-South dialogue and
the search for a new international economic order.

World Religions and the NIEO, contribution of WCRP Netherlands
to the III Assembly of the World Conference on Religion and
Peace in Princeton, August-September 1979.

Part 3 of this document deals with "new style of life and the
new international economic order."

Who works and who doesn't, Boston Industrial Mission, 1979.

An educational packet on labour problems and unemployment in the
USA. The new work ethic and the full employment issue. The
Boston Industrial Mission is an ecumenical centre promoting just
use of increasingly scarce resources to meet human needs. The
main issues of focus are unemployment, economic and environmental
justice, food and development, and theology and the economy.

1979 Conference Report, National Conference on Religion and
Labor, 16-18 May 1979, Washington. Report published by the Center
of Concern.

The people present saw signs of danger for our society in the
coming decade. They spoke of the rise of a New Right, of sustained high unemployment and sustained high inflation aggravating
each other, of runaway shops and new anti-union political offen-
sives, and of political confusion and spiritual hunger in America.
On the positive side, the conference started an ongoing process
of reflection. There were four workshops: 1. religion and labour
in the South today, 2. steelworkers organizing, 2. the permanent
underclass, 4. women: a present challenge.

Third World Development: Challenge for Christians, Board of
Church and Society of the United Methodist Church, "Engage/Social
Action", Washington, D.C., November 1979.

A special 72-page edition, with contributions on: the development
gap; how to make the existing order more just; the roots of
hunger; multinational corporations and development; poverty in
the world; women; global resources mismanagement; citizen action
and church action on development.

No More Plastic Jesus: Global Justice and Christian Lifestyle, by Adam Finnerty, Churchmouse Collective, 1977, 233 pp.

Analysis of the global social/economic situation, the Church's relationship to it, and a vision and strategy for a just world from a Christian perspective.


Energy for My Neighbour Packet of materials, by the World Council of Churches, Geneva, 1978, English, booklet 32 pp. + signposts card for saving, + Appeal to WCC Member Churches, 4 pp.

Ethics of global solidarity and responsible use of world's energetic resources, suggested action programme for the rich countries, implementation of the programme in developing countries.


Dr. Wilhelm Wille, Arbeitsbericht des Evangelischen Missionswerkes, in: epd-Dokumentation, 30 January 1980, German, 28 pp.

Report of the Evangelical Mission Society to the EKD Synod at Garmisch-Partenkirchen, January 1980. An urgent appeal to Western Churches to accept redistribution of wealth, a life style of just participation which is anti-exploitative, anti-military, anti-racist. Evangelical love entails political action, a just New International Economic Order requires a restructuring of Western systems of production and consumption, and also a restructuring of power sharing within Western states, nations, societies.


Living More Simply. Biblical Principles and Practical Models, edited by Ronald J. Sider, Inter-Varsity Press, Downers Grove, Illinois 60515, USA, 1980, 206 pp.

This volume collects the papers presented at the U.S. Consultation on Simple Lifestyle convened at the Overseas Ministries Study Center in Ventnor, New Jersey, April 25-29, 1979. The topics range from the New and Old Testament foundations for simple living to contemporary economics, professional ethics and evangelism. Many personal pilgrimages are detailed as well as the inner workings of numerous fellowship communities and churches.


Radical Christians: What Has Happened to Them? What Lies Ahead?, published by the Joint Strategic and Action Committee, a coalition of the "national mission" agencies of the major Protestant denominations in the United States, New York, May 1980.

History and perspectives of "Theology in the Americas" as it gathers in Detroit for its second full conference of assessment. The issues facing the movement: economic and political change 1975-1980; the future of minorities; women in Church and Society; American liberalism; looking for an economic alternative.

Christian Commitment for the '80s. Study/Action Guides for Social Change, by Inter-Religious Task Force for Social Analysis. Available from the New York Circus, P.O. Box 37, Times Square Station, New York, N.Y. 10036, USA.

Vol. 1, 1979, 128 pp., Must We Choose Side?, explores the role of working people in our economic system; investigates harsh realities of everyday life. Who owns America? Who pays the price? Six comprehensive sessions help readers examine class background and the myths of capitalism.

Vol. 2, 1980, 200 pp., Which Side Are We On?, deepens our understanding of the present crisis - inflation, unemployment, the danger of war. Moves beyond historical critique of capitalism to explore other alternatives. Raises questions for Christian activists: Can we reclaim our radical heritage? How do we confront political and religious ideology?